GATINEAU PARK

An Intimate Portrait

Sugar maple, beech and white oak leaves on King Mountain.

GATINEAU PARK

An Intimate Portrait

J. DAVID ANDREWS

WILDLIFE PAINTINGS BY BRENDA CARTER

FOREWORD BY FREEMAN PATTERSON

DYNAMIC LIGHT

Acknowledgments

For their invaluable assistance in preparing the text
of this book, I would like to thank my friend Max Finkelstein
and my editor Brenda Missen.

Published by Dynamic Light Productions
1890 Wembley Avenue
Ottawa, Ontario K2A 1A7

Canadian Cataloguing in Publication Data
Andrews, J. David, 1961-
      Gatineau Park : an intimate portrait

Includes bibliographical references.
ISBN 0-9697013-0-6

1. Gatineau Park (Quebec). 2. Gatineau Park
(Quebec) — Pictorial works. I. Carter, Brenda
II. Title.

FC2914.G38A64 1994 917.14'221 C93-090163-0
F1054.G28A64 1994

Design: Brant Cowie/ArtPlus Limited.

Printed in Korea by Dong-A Publishing and Printing Company, Ltd.

Contents

Foreword

Everything takes time — singing a song, writing a letter, creating a book, shopping, eating, sleeping, seeing, thinking. When we are young we wish time would hurry up, but as we grow older we wish it would slow down. However, the centuries, years, months, days, hours, and minutes — human signposts that mark the continuum of eternity — seem long or short depending not only on how old we are, but also on who or what we are. A worker bee that lives a long time will die within a few weeks, a person celebrating an 80th birthday is living on "borrowed time," a glacier may advance for thousands of years and then retreat for thousands more, the universe is 16 billion years old and still growing. Perhaps it is only an adolescent. We have a concept of time because we recognize change. No change, no concept of time. History is about the flow of change and about completed, usually sequential, changes. It's also about the pacing of these changes — slower or faster — and the impact that the rate of change has had on subsequent events.

In his text for this book, David Andrews documents the long flow of change (by human measurement) and specific changes in the area we now call Gatineau Park. His description evokes the perceptions of time experienced during the various stages of a human life: a childhood that, from the child's perspective, seemed to last forever; the change and time gradually speeding up as the first people traversed the region; the last 400 years, when time began to race by as Europeans drastically altered the face of the land. He leaves us in the present, asking the question: What lies in the future for Gatineau Park?

David Andrews' photographs provide his answer — the one he hopes for. His images are loving documents and impressions of the past-that-exists-in-the-present. They acknowledge a place for humans in Gatineau Park, but collectively make the point that a future without wildness will be a denial of the past. His pictures show the community of natural elements and living things which were and still are Gatineau Park. They make us think and they make us feel. They ascribe value — ecologically and spiritually.

In the late 20th century perhaps the most distinguishing feature of our species is our ability to comprehend Earth as a single, living entity. We are the first and currently the only species in the planet's history that can exercise a global perspective.

Bunchberry flowers near Lac la Pêche.

We can see the "connectedness" between all regions of the globe, between all ecosystems, and between all living and non-living things. We can observe how the condition of one area or ecosystem ultimately affects Earth's entire body. And we have the knowledge and the technology to keep Earth healthy. But do we have the will?

David Andrews is one person who does. He believes that an individual — he, you, and I — can make a difference. He undertook this book project because he cares deeply for Gatineau Park, and because he understands its planetary context. Through his words and photographs *he speaks for Gatineau Park and for Earth —* and on behalf of everybody who believes and feels as he does.

FREEMAN PATTERSON

Preface

My earliest memories of Gatineau Park are of fumbling to secure my boots into uncooperative ski bindings, of frozen fingers and toes, and of following my mother's purple knickers through the forest. I remember being somewhat less than enthusiastic about these weekend ski outings. The entire escapade seemed to be a lot of trouble for a little suffering. However, as I grew, my attitude improved. Eventually I learned how to keep my fingers warm in winter, and it was not long before I was leaving my mother behind to care for my younger brother while I explored the Gatineau forests in earnest.

A bicycle, and later a motorcycle, replaced my skis during summer. Where the pavement ended, hiking boots and running shoes carried me deeper into the Gatineau forests, sometimes for days at a time.

As the years passed, my fascination with the natural world grew, and photography became the medium through which I explored it. I travelled farther afield, spending summers working as a guide, exploring spectacular wilderness areas in Canada's north. But even as I paddled down remote wilderness rivers, drinking from crystal clear streams within sight of grizzly bear and wolverine, my mind often drifted back to the subtle beauty and charm of Gatineau Park: the cheerful song of a chickadee; leaves rustling on a warm summer breeze; the brilliant colours of autumn; the odour of moist earth and leaves on the forest floor in spring; and the sensations of skiing alone through the woods, a cold wind on my cheeks, the sound of woodpeckers drumming, the crackle of frozen trees and the exhilaration of a perfect run down Highland Trail to Kingsmere.

During the drive home after a long hike, on a particularly cold, wet November afternoon in 1988, a friend and I discussed the idea of creating a book that would celebrate Gatineau Park through words and photographs. What followed was a journey of discovery, an exploration of the beauty and mystery of the natural world and of the sense of wonder to be experienced in my own backyard.

I remember a night when the air was so still and cold and the silence so complete that, when I walked, the crunch of snow under my feet sent sound waves crashing through the forest. I felt alone, but imagined that all around me were animals whose ears perked up to the noise. Suddenly the howl of a distant wolf drifted across the lake and, in response, a chorus of whines and howls erupted only a few metres away.

Reflection of standing deadwood and autumn foliage.

There were countless early mornings and thousands of hours of searching for that one elusive image that would capture the very essence of Gatineau Park. Of course I never found that image, but I hope that through the photographs that appear in this book I share with you the sense of wonder, and the joy of discovery, that I experienced in creating them. Together with the text, and Brenda's wonderful paintings, they provide an intimate portrait of the forests, hills, valleys, lakes and streams that we call Gatineau Park.

The establishment and preservation of Gatineau Park has been an ongoing struggle ever since the park was first proposed in 1903. This book is dedicated to all those who have fought that struggle, and especially to those who continue to sacrifice their time and energy to ensure the integrity of Gatineau Park's wildness.

J. DAVID ANDREWS

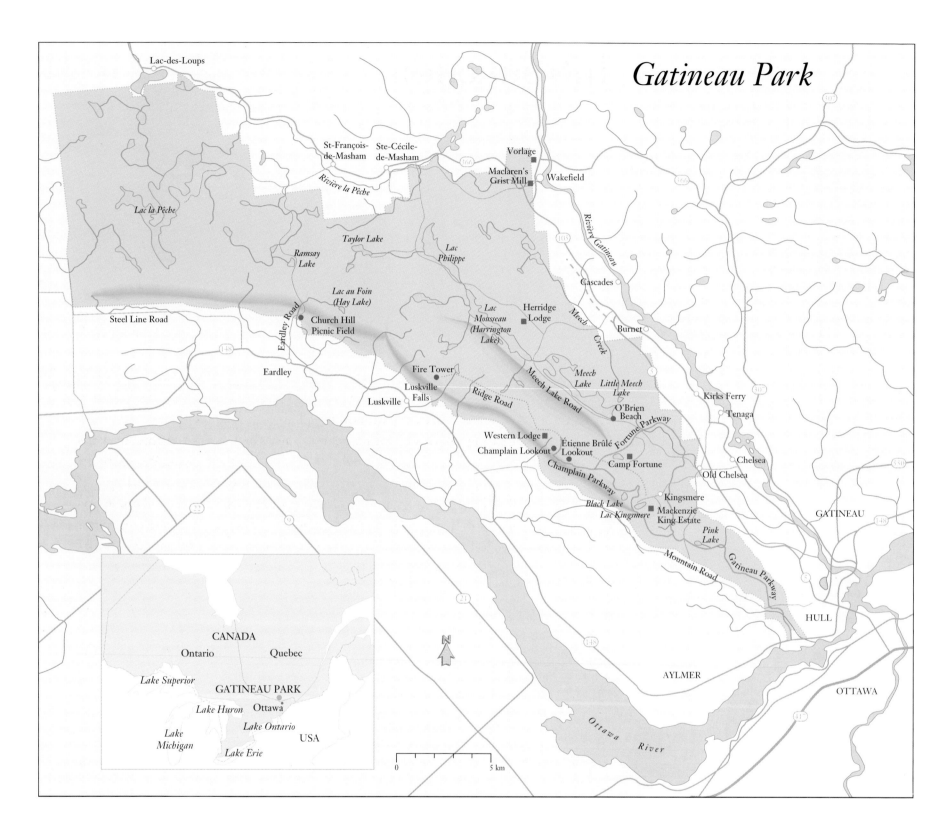

Gatineau Park

Lac-des-Loups

St-François-de-Masham   Ste-Cécile-de-Masham

Vorlage

Maclaren's Grist Mill   Wakefield

Rivière la Pêche

Lac la Pêche

Taylor Lake

Lac Philippe

Ramsay Lake

Rivière Gatineau

Cascades

Lac au Foin (Hay Lake)

Steel Line Road

Church Hill Picnic Field

Lac Mousseau (Harrington Lake)

Herridge Lodge

Burnet

Meech Creek

Eardley

Eardley Road

Fire Tower

Luskville Falls

Luskville

Ridge Road

Meech Lake Road

Meech Lake

Little Meech Lake

Kirks Ferry

Tenaga

O'Brien Beach

Western Lodge

Champlain Lookout

Étienne Brûlé Lookout

Fortune Parkway

Camp Fortune

Chelsea

Old Chelsea

Champlain Parkway

Kingsmere

Black Lake
Lac Kingsmere

Mackenzie King Estate

GATINEAU

Pink Lake

Mountain Road

Gatineau Parkway

HULL

CANADA

Ontario   Quebec

Lake Superior

GATINEAU PARK

Ottawa

Lake Huron

Lake Ontario

USA

Lake Michigan

Lake Erie

AYLMER

OTTAWA

Ottawa River

N

0   5 km

Introduction

Gatineau Park encompasses roughly thirty-five thousand hectares in Quebec's Gatineau Hills, an oasis of wilderness on the doorstep of Canada's national capital. This is quintessential Canadian Shield country, a land of rolling hills dotted with picturesque lakes and beaver ponds, pink rock outcrops and polychrome forests of maple, beech, birch and pine.

These forests are home to a remarkable diversity of wildlife, including deer, bears and even timber wolves, yet they are also the backyard playground for a metropolitan population of over a million people.

On a sunny spring afternoon, while beavers busy themselves reinforcing dams against meltwater floods, and great blue herons refurbish their nests, the southern tip of the park bustles with human activity. Cyclists and roller skiers whirl up and down the winding hills of the Champlain and Fortune parkways and hikers disappear into a maze of forest trails. At the Mackenzie King Estate, tourists sip tea in the dining room of the former Prime Minister's summer home and explore his extraordinary collection of ruins while strolling among flower gardens and woodland trails.

In the heat of summer, people's attention turns to the park's lakes for swimming, picnicking and camping. Along the Eardley Escarpment, rock climbers scramble up granite cliffs and hang-gliders launch themselves from atop King Mountain to soar on updraughts high above the Ottawa Valley. When the summer sun begins to fade, the Gatineau hillsides erupt in a riot of colour that draws painters, photographers and sightseers by the thousands.

By November the leaves have fallen, the parkways are closed, the beaches are deserted, and the forest trails see only a few hardy hikers and mountain bikers. Then the snow comes and once again people flock to hillsides and forest trails to enjoy some of the best cross-country skiing in eastern Canada.

Gatineau Park has an extraordinary history. The hills themselves are roots of ancient mountains, formed almost a billion years ago. The park forests have a history of change and development that dates back twelve thousand years to a time when an ancient sea washed against the Eardley Escarpment.

As long ago as seven thousand years, Canada's first peoples hunted, fished, and traded copper and flint throughout the region. In 1613 Samuel de Champlain paddled

past the park, opening up the Ottawa River as an important route for explorers and fur traders travelling west. Two centuries later, American and European immigrants built homesteads and planted crops on park lands. Their farms were soon abandoned, and the fields, so laboriously cleared, have been reclaimed by the forest.

During the 1930s, when the Gatineau Hills were being stripped of their forests for fuel and pulpwood, public indignation spurred the creation of Gatineau Park. Management of the park, a balancing act between preserving its wilderness character and catering to the ever-increasing demands for outdoor recreation, is the responsibility of the National Capital Commission, an organization that manages federal government properties in the National Capital Region.

There are no towering mountains, mile-deep canyons or spectacular white-water rivers in Gatineau Park. Nothing here is the highest, deepest, biggest or rarest. But it is a land of subtle beauty, charm and grace.

Butternut tree and stream on the Eardley Escarpment.

Natural History

THE EMERGENCE OF THE HILLS

Along the southern boundary of Gatineau Park, the cliffs of the Eardley Escarpment rise abruptly out of the rolling plain of the Ottawa Valley. From the time the first American settlers arrived on the banks of the Ottawa and Gatineau rivers over two hundred years ago, these cliffs have served as a barrier helping to preserve the natural beauty of the Gatineau Hills. On the ridge above the escarpment, the fertile soils that carpet the Ottawa Valley are nowhere to be found. In their place, sparse oak forests and grassy meadows cling to the exposed bedrock. To the northeast, a series of knobby hills covered with forests of maple, beech and pine, and dotted with dozens of small lakes and beaver ponds, descend toward the line of lakes Philippe, Harrington and Meech. These rugged hills are part of the Canadian Shield, the bedrock of our nation, and they are the wilderness heart of Gatineau Park. This land evokes a sense of tranquillity and permanence — a serenity that belies an extraordinary history of great physical turmoil and change, a history that explains much about the landscape of Gatineau Park today.

The Gatineau Hills are remnants of the ancient Laurentian Mountains, formed almost a billion years ago when the only life-forms on the planet were anaerobic bacteria, slime molds, fungi and clumps of blue-green algae. Earth is similar in structure to an egg. The interior of the planet is molten; around the surface is a thin shell, a crust of hard rock. Unlike an egg's shell, however, Earth's crust is divided into discrete pieces known as "tectonic plates." Like pack ice drifting on the ocean, these tectonic plates move about, albeit very slowly, and collide with one another, exerting tremendous forces on Earth's crust. As a result, rocks become crushed and folded and mountains are thrust up. At the same time that rock is forced upward to form peaks, it is also forced downward into Earth's soft, molten layers to form the roots of mountains.

It was among the roots of the Laurentian Mountains that the rocks of the Gatineau Hills were formed. Many kilometres below Earth's surface, the mountain roots were subjected to great pressure and intense heat. They became soft and began to flow, like peanut butter that has been left out in the sun. Under these conditions, sedimentary rocks such as limestone and sandstone that had been formed on the bottom of ancient seas were changed into marble and quartzite. Some rocks became hot enough to form molten magma, which made its way up through cracks in the overlying rock. Where it reached the surface, volcanoes erupted, spewing forth fiery lava.

Evidence of these events is visible throughout the park. A good example can be seen in the rock cut opposite Black Lake on the Champlain Parkway. Here the dominant greyish rock is gneiss, the most common rock type in the park. Running through the gneiss are streaks of pink rock. These streaks, called "dykes," are a mixture of quartz and pink microcline feldspar. As molten magma, these minerals made their way into cracks in the gneiss where they later cooled and crystallized, deep within the planet, over six hundred million years ago.

Long before the Rocky Mountains or the Appalachians existed, the Laurentians were a mighty mountain range, yet as soon as they began to rise, the inevitable forces of erosion began to wear them down. Each time it rained, soluble material in the rock was dissolved and carried away in the runoff. Rivulets and streams carried small particles of stone and pebbles that wore down the bedrock like sandpaper. Fine particles picked up by the wind etched exposed surfaces. Water that froze in cracks expanded, splitting the rock as surely as an axe splits a piece of cordwood, exposing new surfaces to the unrelenting forces of wind and rain. Particle by particle, the wind and water gradually wore down and carried the mountains away. As the weight of the overlying rock was reduced, the Gatineau Hills, ever so slowly, rose to the surface.

No sooner had the mountain roots reached the surface than they were buried again. During the Ordovician Era, from approximately five hundred to four hundred and twenty-five million years ago, what is now southern Quebec and eastern Ontario was flooded by seven successive oceans. Sediment settling to the floor of these ancient seas eventually covered the Gatineau Hills, transforming the land into a vast, featureless plain.

The land might have remained a plain to this day had it not been for the tremendous tectonic upheaval that created the Eardley Escarpment. Almost two hundred million years after the last of the Ordovician seas had drained away, the tectonic plate that supports the European continent collided with the North American plate. The force of this collision warped and folded Earth's crust, pushing up the Appalachian Mountains and causing enormous cracks known as "faults" to form throughout what is now Ontario, Quebec and the north-eastern United States. Eventually a huge block of Earth's crust dropped down along a series of parallel faults to form the Ottawa-St. Lawrence Lowlands, a valley that stretches from the Eardley Escarpment a hundred kilometres south into New York State and as far east as Quebec City. A lesser fault created the depression within which lies the chain of lakes, Philippe, Harrington and Meech.

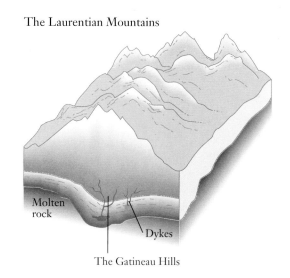

The Laurentian Mountains

Molten rock

Dykes

The Gatineau Hills

600 million years ago

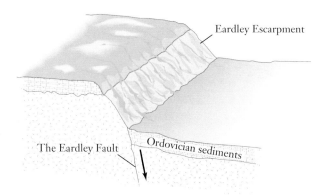

Formation of the Eardley Escarpment

Eardley Escarpment

The Eardley Fault

Ordovician sediments

270 million years ago

The sedimentary deposits laid down during the Ordovician Era form the limestone and sandstone bedrock that has been preserved throughout much of the Ottawa Valley and western Quebec. However, in the highlands to the north, exposure to millions of years of erosion, and to glaciation during several ice ages, has worn away these soft sedimentary rocks, leaving the roots of the ancient Laurentian Mountains exposed.

THE AGE OF ICE

When the weather becomes cold enough so that the snow that falls each winter does not completely melt away each summer, snow begins to pile up, deeper and deeper, year after year, until its weight transforms the lower layers into ice. As snow and ice continue to accumulate, an enormous ice sheet forms. Eventually, the weight at the centre of the sheet becomes so great that the ice at the margins begins to spread outward or to "advance," similar to the way pastry dough spreads out under the weight of a rolling pin. Four times during the last hundred thousand years great ice sheets have advanced out of the north. The most recent advance, known as the Wisconsin Glaciation, lasted thirty thousand years and retreated only twelve thousand years ago. At its peak, Gatineau Park was covered with a blanket of ice over two kilometres thick!

The effects of the ice age are clearly visible throughout Gatineau Park. The glaciers scoured the landscape over which they travelled, at first scraping off soil and loose rock, then using that material, like a giant sanding block, to grind the bedrock. Huge volumes of rock were ground up and carried great distances within the ice. As the ice melted and the glaciers receded, the debris they were carrying was left behind, scattered across the landscape. The retreat of the glaciers, however, was not uniform; minor fluctuations in the weather caused them at times to surge forward or to remain static. When a glacier is static, the ice may continue to spread outward from the centre, but it does not appear to advance or retreat because the rate of growth is equalled by the rate of melt at the margins. When this happens, rock and boulders released by the melting ice collect in mounds called "moraines" around the outer edge of the glacier.

Meech Lake once drained south through Chelsea Creek until the moraine upon which O'Brien Beach is situated blocked its path. As this moraine formed, a block of ice separated from the glacier and was buried within the moraine. As the block melted, it left a hollow or "kettle," a deep depression in the landscape. This kettle is clearly visible just to the left of Meech Lake Road as you approach the lake from the O'Brien Beach parking lot.

Along the ridge above the Eardley Escarpment, deep scratches are visible in the exposed bedrock, scoured out by chunks of rock being dragged across the landscape

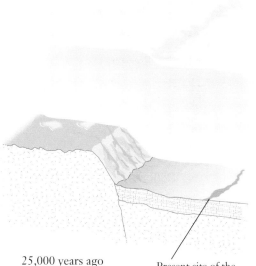

The Wisconsin Glaciation

25,000 years ago

Present site of the Ottawa River

at the base of the moving ice sheet. Boulders of various sizes called "erratics," gouged from mountains to the north and carried by the glaciers, are found throughout the park, dropped unceremoniously in valleys and on ridge tops.

The tremendous weight of the Wisconsin ice sheet depressed Earth's crust several hundred metres into the planet's soft molten layers. Consequently, as the ice melted, the Atlantic Ocean reached up into the St. Lawrence River Valley as far west as the present site of Pembroke. For two thousand years, the high ground in Gatineau Park formed a peninsula jutting out into this ancient arm of the Atlantic known as the Champlain Sea. Low-lying areas, including the southern tip of the park near the City of Hull and the major lakes la Pêche, Philippe, Harrington and Meech were all submerged. The flag-pole on top of the Peace Tower would have been just under the water's surface.

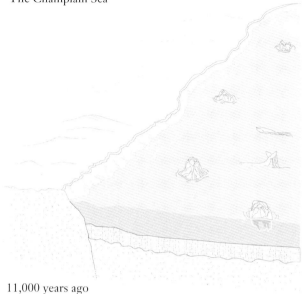

11,000 years ago

THE COMING OF THE FORESTS

In the early years of the Champlain Sea, a towering wall of ice loomed over its northern shore. The sea was frozen over much of the year, and pack ice and icebergs choked its waters during summer. The part of present-day Gatineau Park that was above sea level was a formidable place. Gale force winds off the glacier whipped up clouds of fine rock particles, sand and snow, carrying them across a hard, barren landscape strewn with piles of rock and ice.

Into this harsh environment came the earliest pioneers of the Gatineau forests. Lichen, arriving as spores borne on the wind, were the first life-forms to colonize the bare rock. Lichen are actually a partnership between two different organisms — fungi and algae. Through the magic of photosynthesis, the algae produce organic matter upon which the fungus feeds. The fungus produces acids that break down and release nutrients from the rock to which it adheres, and provides physical structure to the lichen, exposing the algae to sunlight like the leaves of a tree.

The organic matter produced by the lichens provided the nourishment necessary for mosses and grasses to become established. As generations of these plants grew and died back, fine wind-blown particles settled among the protection of their roots and a thin layer of soil and humus developed, softening the land's surface. Eventually a dense blanket of vegetation covered the landscape, trapping heat and creating a micro-environment several degrees warmer than the air temperature. Thriving in this habitat were herbs and shrubs, extending only a few inches above the ground, and a profusion of tiny colourful flowers, such as arctic poppies, cotton grass and lapland rhododendron.

As the climate warmed, the ice sheet melted and, relieved of its burden of ice, the land began slowly to rebound, causing the Champlain Sea to drain eastward into the Atlantic Ocean. In the Gatineau Hills, a few stunted white spruce trees, the vanguard of the boreal forest, began to emerge from the tundra.

The Penny Ice Cap, a six thousand square-kilometre expanse of ice on Baffin Island in the Canadian Arctic, is a remnant of the last great ice sheet that once covered much of North America. The ice there is still retreating and life is recolonizing the land, as it did in Gatineau Park twelve thousand years ago. A few kilometres south of the ice, a tundra community has developed, and farther south, in northern Ontario and Quebec, the tundra has given way to boreal forest as it once did in Gatineau Park.

Generations of spruce forest enriched the soil in the Gatineau Hills, providing a seedbed for less hardy species that were spreading northward more slowly from their ice age refuge in the south-eastern United States. Eventually balsam fir, birch, oak, and red and white pine became established throughout the region. As much as a thousand years later, eastern hemlock arrived and flourished as a dominant species for many generations before being all but wiped out, possibly by a fungus or insect infestation, around five thousand years ago. In its place, a mixed forest of conifers and hardwoods became established: maple, birch and beech, along with a few hemlock and great stands of red and white pine. This was the forest that greeted the first American and European settlers to the Ottawa River Valley. Sadly, nearly all the pines were cut down for the square timber trade in the 1800s, and by 1940 much of the remaining hardwood forest had been cleared for lumber or firewood.

Today, small stands of hemlock still grow on a few north-facing slopes, while balsam fir, spruce, birch and aspen flourish in low-lying areas, such as along the Eardley Road. However, throughout most of Gatineau Park, sugar maple and beech have established themselves as the dominant species.

The canopy of the sugar maple-beech forest cuts out as much as ninety percent of sunlight, creating an environment in which only the most shade tolerant trees can survive. Basswood and red oak are common, although the red oaks require a considerable amount of sunlight and will likely become rare as the forest matures. Ironwood, red and white pine, spruce, birch, balsam fir and hemlock also grow throughout the forest but are less common. Early in the season, before the canopy blocks out the sunlight, the forest floor hosts a magnificent display of hundreds of thousands of trilliums, as well as spring beauties, trout lilies, wild ginger, large-flowered bellwort and an abundance of other wildflowers.

The many old farm fields and cleared areas in the park are a kaleidoscope of colour from April to October as thousands of wildflowers compete for sunlight and soil nutrients. Even as the last patches of snow linger in the forest, the tiny white flowers of wild strawberries begin to emerge in the field undergrowth. On their heels come the many brightly coloured blossoms of spring, including buttercups, Canada anemone and the beautiful blue flag iris. The warm breezes of summer arouse entire fields of daisies, and hawkweed of yellow and orange, to an elegant dance. When the ferns begin to change colour in September and October, the greens of summer fields turn to a thousand shades of yellow, gold and brown, accented by the pastel blooms of goldenrod, asters and pearly everlasting.

These fields are also undergoing more subtle changes from year to year as they develop into mature woods. In some, sumac and juniper have begun to shade out the grasses and flowers, while around the perimeter of many, fast growing trembling aspen and birch have taken root. These trees thrive in direct sunlight, but the shade they provide actually hinders the growth of their own seedlings, while providing a healthy environment for more shade tolerant young sugar maple and beech trees. A band of this transition forest is clearly visible around many open areas bordering the Gatineau Parkway. Young birch and aspen, at the leading edge of the forest, slowly encroach into the fields, while a few metres back taller trees are being overtaken by the advance of the maples. Eventually maple and beech will completely shade out the pioneering species.

The south-facing cliffs of the Eardley Escarpment support a unique habitat that is strikingly different from the rest of the park. Protected from cold northern winds and receiving maximum exposure to sunlight, the escarpment maintains a hot, dry micro-climate and an extended growing season. These conditions allow for the growth of southern species such as sicklepod, blunt-lobed woodsia and walking fern — three primarily Appalachian species either absent or rare elsewhere in the region. Steep rock faces separate patches of open forest where red oak grow alongside southern species such as white oak, hackberry and red juniper. Between the trees and within crevices in the rock grow grasses, blueberries and wild columbine — plants that prefer a well drained soil and lots of sunshine. Thin soil and strong winds stunt growth on the escarpment. Although the trees are small, many are over one hundred years old.

Exploring the King Mountain Trail

Let your imagination come with me for a stroll around the King Mountain Trail to explore some of the Gatineau Park forests of the past, present and future. From the Black Lake parking lot we will head west up the hill beside the lake, to where the trail passes through a dense stand of hemlocks growing in a rich, moist soil shaded from the sun by the steep north-facing slope. Notice the litter of chewed cones dropped to the floor by the squirrels who tunnel out their nests amongst the tree roots. Are these squirrels descendants of others who foraged among the hemlock forests that flourished in Gatineau Park six thousand years ago?

On top of the mountain, the trail skirts the crest of the escarpment where an open forest of stunted red and white oak overlooks the Ottawa River Valley.

Farther along, as the trail winds back down the mountain, we pass through a mature maple forest containing trees that are nearly two hundred years old. This grove is a rare example of the hardwood forest that flourished throughout the region only a few decades ago and reflects the character of the Gatineau Park of the future as the present forest matures. Sift through the layer of litter on the forest floor; this is where insects and mites begin the process of decomposing organic material by chewing tiny holes in the leaves. As we dig down, notice how the leaves appear darker and are coated with a slimy film of microscopic fungi and bacteria. Deeper still, the leaves become increasingly skeletonized until we reach the dark moist layer that makes up the humus. Pick up some in your hands, smell its rich musty fragrance, let it fall between your fingers. This is the legacy of the future, the storehouse of nutrients that powers the cycle of life in the forests of Gatineau Park. Imagine the molecules hidden within this handful of earth. Were they once a part of the tundra that grew here when the Champlain Sea splashed against King Mountain, or were they part of a young Algonkin who hunted in these hills a thousand years before Europeans arrived? What kinds of plants and animals will they become a part of in the future?

STILL WILD AFTER ALL THESE YEARS

If we sit on the crest of the Eardley Escarpment on a spring morning, we will likely hear a red squirrel scurrying among last year's dried leaves in its search for acorns; or see a red-tailed hawk soaring on an updraught as it hunts for mice in the fields below. For a moment, try to imagine that we are looking out from this same high perch eleven thousand years ago. In the valley before us, a pod of beluga whales is frolicking in the Champlain Sea. The morning sun glistens off the water, forcing us to shield our eyes and squint as we watch bowhead and humpback whales surfacing in the distance. Close to shore, a colony of bearded seals is diving after a school of sculpin, while sea birds search for caplin and sticklebacks in the surface waters. If this were February, harp seals would be gathering on pack ice at the foot of King Mountain to give birth to hundreds of white coated pups with adorable "frying pan" eyes, as they do in the Gulf of St. Lawrence today. Nearby, a motionless snowshoe hare watches nervously as a pine marten inches its way along the trunk of a fallen spruce tree, silently closing the gap between itself and an unsuspecting eastern chipmunk.

Today the valley before us is a mosaic of roads, farm fields, sprawling suburbs and strip-malls, but all that stops at the base of the escarpment. Like an impenetrable barrier to human progress, the escarpment has helped preserve the primeval wilderness of the Gatineau forests. Follow me as we turn our backs on the hustle and bustle below, and walk into a forest where eastern chipmunk, snowshoe hare and the rare pine marten still live. Notice how cool and moist the air is under the canopy of maple and beech leaves. A thick layer of soil, the legacy of ancient forests, fills in every dip and valley in the bedrock. Beneath our feet, moles, shrews and voles live out their lives in a world completely hidden from our eyes. Peek under an old fallen tree and we may discover a pair of blue-spotted salamanders or a nest of tiny redbelly snakes. Ahead, a drumming sound, low at first but rising quickly in tempo and volume, emanates from a small grove of spruce trees. As we pass the grove, a ruffed grouse bolts out, a mass of feathers and anxiety that almost takes off our kneecaps on its way by. On cold winter nights, this grouse will plunge into the soft upper layers of the snow, tunnelling a short distance before carving out a cavity in which to spend the night. Here the bird can rest comfortably, protected from the bitter cold by an insulating blanket of snow.

Ahead the ground slopes downward to where sunlight is piercing through the trees at the edge of a beaver pond. At one end of the pond, several deer graze in a grassy meadow, except for one large doe who stands alert, staring intently in our direction. A pair of black ducks, looking as if they have lost something, swim nervously around in circles near the far shore. A kingfisher, disturbed by our presence, lets out a raspy cry and flies to a branch overlooking the far side of the pond. As we turn and walk along the shoreline, our movement spooks the watchful doe, and half a dozen deer bound into the forest, flashing the white underside of their tails as they go.

The beaver dam that holds back this pond is several metres long and over two metres wide. Its thick covering of grass indicates that it has been here for many years. We are in a long sloping valley interspersed with marshland and beaver ponds, and this dam forms a convenient bridge to the opposite side. As we step across, we are engulfed by a mass of cold air resting above the pond — a reminder that winter lingers late in the forest. Only a trickle of water gurgles through the mass of sticks and mud beneath our feet. In the swampy meadow on the opposite side of the dam, a chorus of spring peepers and wood frogs announces the coming of spring, while red-winged blackbirds, marsh wrens and swamp sparrows flirt among the bulrushes.

Throughout Gatineau Park, hundreds of similar swamps and ponds provide habitat for thousands of creatures: river otters, muskrats, several species of turtle, osprey, great blue herons and a multitude of songbirds. In the large lakes, loons dive for perch and speckled trout. Porcupine, black bear and red fox share the forests with such rare species as fisher, ermine and mink. Even timber wolves, a symbol of the very essence of primeval wilderness, are occasionally spotted in the remote western regions of the park. This is Gatineau Park's greatest and most endangered treasure, its wildness.

PINK LAKE: A HIDDEN TIME CAPSULE

Gatineau Park has its share of remarkable natural features, but Pink Lake stands out not only for its beauty but for its unique ecology. The lake is named after Samuel Pink, who settled nearby in 1826. For many years, settlers living along the Mountain Road cut ice blocks from the lake to keep their food fresh in summer. At the time they could not have guessed at the extraordinary history and unusual life-forms associated with the lake.

During the 1970s it was discovered that Pink Lake is one of only a handful of lakes in Canada that are meromictic. A meromictic lake is one in which the water does not circulate throughout the basin but instead remains stratified year-round. In a typical lake, the water completely mixes each spring and fall as surface and bottom temperatures reach an equilibrium. The turn-over of waters replenishes oxygen and nutrients to the deeper areas. In Pink Lake the water mixes only to a depth of thirteen metres. Below this depth, millions of tiny mineral particles and dissolved salts increase the water's density, and, like an oil and vinegar salad dressing, the two layers do not mix. The upper portion of the water column rests on a seven-metre deep pool of heavier water, which is isolated from the surface and completely without oxygen.

The absence of oxygen prevents organic material on the lake bottom from decomposing. Pollen grains retrieved from these sediments provide a record of the vegetation that grew around the lake dating back to the time of the Champlain Sea.

The deep waters of Pink Lake are home to one of the planet's earliest life-forms — bacteria capable of photosynthesizing food energy from sunlight without oxygen. The bacteria congregate at the top of the oxygen-free zone, forming a dense cloud through which no light penetrates.

Pink Lake is also home to a tiny fish called the three-spined stickleback, a living relic of the Champlain Sea. Sticklebacks are common in both salt and fresh water, although physiologically the two groups are quite different. The sticklebacks living in Pink Lake are unique. Although they live in fresh water, they are more closely related to saltwater sticklebacks than they are to other freshwater populations. Following the retreat of the Champlain Sea, the transition from salt water to fresh water in most park lakes took only a few decades and saltwater fish species died off. In meromictic Pink Lake, the transition took three thousand years, long enough for the three-spined stickleback to adapt to fresh water.

After ten thousand years of development, Pink Lake's unique ecology is now threatened. During summer, high concentrations of algae give the lake a green cast. The white rock seen in the cliffs around the lake is rich in phosphate, a natural fertilizer that nourishes algae growth. During the 1970s, the wear and tear of thousands of people walking on the easily eroded bedrock resulted in a tremendous

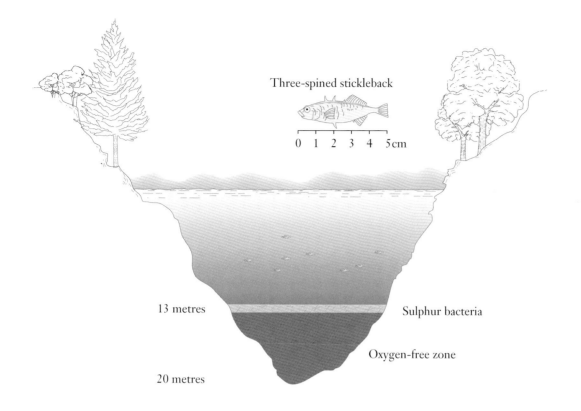

Three-spined stickleback

0 1 2 3 4 5cm

13 metres

Sulphur bacteria

Oxygen-free zone

20 metres

increase in the amount of phosphorous washed into the lake. The high phosphate levels caused algae blooms, which threatened to upset the lake's fragile ecological balance. In the 1980s an extensive rehabilitation campaign was undertaken to combat phosphate contamination. Thousands of trees were planted around the lake to reduce erosion, and boardwalks were built to minimize visitor impact. Recently, the disappearance of several individuals, all of whom were last seen tramping about off the established trail, has led to speculation that a ferocious monster lives in the lake, waiting to devour anyone who defies the rehabilitation effort. Unconfirmed sightings suggest the elusive creature is at least seven metres long, has twelve rows of enormous, razor-sharp teeth and, at last report, looked very hungry. Stay on the path!

Human History

THE FIRST PEOPLES

Imagine Gatineau Park eleven thousand years ago. The Gatineau Hills are a narrow peninsula of barren rock. To the north, the land is buried beneath an enormous ice sheet; to the south, waves of the Champlain Sea break against the face of the Eardley Escarpment. Farther south, across the Champlain Sea, the first Americans — descendants of peoples who crossed the land bridge between Siberia and Alaska twenty thousand years earlier — collect birds' eggs and berries, and hunt caribou, mammoths and mastodons in a sub-arctic environment.

As time passed, the Champlain Sea gradually receded eastward, enabling animals, as well as the people who depended on them, to move north. As long ago as seven thousand years, descendants of these first Americans, tribes of nomadic hunters whom archaeologists call the Laurentian Archaic Culture, lived in what is now southern Ontario and Quebec. They collected the nuts, berries and roots of many plants, used hooks and harpoons to catch fish, and hunted elk, deer, beaver and bear to provide both food and clothing. How often or how many of these people actually set foot within what is now Gatineau Park is impossible to say, but they were certainly close by. The Ottawa River served as a trade route along

Eleven thousand years ago, when Gatineau Park was a narrow peninsula of barren rock, Palaeo-indians hunted caribou, mammoths and mastodons in a sub-arctic environment south of the Champlain Sea.

As the Champlain Sea gradually receded eastward, the climate grew steadily warmer, allowing forests, animals and people to move north. As long ago as seven thousand years, people of the Laurentian Archaic Culture lived in the Ottawa River Valley.

which copper, quartzite, flint and probably furs, food and ideas travelled. Tools unearthed at five-thousand-year-old Laurentian encampments on the Ottawa River include fish-hooks, drills, needles, axes, knives and projectile points made from copper that had been mined along the north shore of Lake Superior; flint, quarried as far away as the Gaspé Peninsula and New York State; and quartzite from northern Labrador. Many bone implements were also found, including barbed harpoons, woodworking tools and a small flute.

The Gatineau River likely served as an important link between the people living in the Ottawa Valley and the people of the Shield Archaic Culture who lived to the north. The Shield Archaic peoples migrated, over a period of thousands of years, into the northern forests of Ontario and Quebec from the western plains. Their home was a land of dense forests, fast-flowing rivers and deep snows. They relied heavily on caribou and moose for food and clothing and are credited with developing both the snowshoe and the birchbark canoe.

By the time the first Europeans arrived in North America, the descendants of the Laurentian Archaic Culture had migrated southward, and Algonkin

Algonkin encampment at the junction of the Desert and Gatineau rivers, circa 1870.

Indians, descendants of the Shield Archaic Culture, occupied the Ottawa and Gatineau river valleys.

The Algonkin cultivated small amounts of maize, squash and beans, but the dense maple, beech and pine forests that grew throughout the region were better suited to a lifestyle of hunting and gathering. The Algonkin collected a rich harvest of flowers, leaves, roots and mushrooms, as well as many fruits and nuts, including blueberries, strawberries, high bush cranberries, acorns and beechnuts. They also trapped and hunted a wide variety of large and small game and often fished at night with a torch held above the water to attract fish within reach of nets and spears. They made dwellings from long poles arranged in teepee fashion or from green boughs stuck into the ground and bent over to form a dome, which they covered with bark or skins. They could easily remove and carry the covering, by canoe or toboggan, to a new site while leaving the frame intact for future use. During summer the Algonkin lived in settlements on the shores of large lakes and rivers, but in winter they dispersed into small family groups spread throughout the forest.

Gatineau Park has no lakes or rivers large or accessible enough to support permanent native settlements. However, small hunting parties undoubtedly travelled within the park. During winter, the Philippe, Harrington and Meech chain of lakes, and the Pêche River, likely allowed easy travel by snowshoe and toboggan, while the sheltered south-facing cliffs of the Eardley Escarpment provided a haven for both wildlife and people, as they do today.

An encampment in the forest.

THE EUROPEAN EXPLORERS

The first European to gaze across the Ottawa Valley to the Gatineau Hills was the young French explorer Étienne Brûlé, after whom a lookout and picnic ground in the park are named. Brûlé came to New France in 1608 at the age of seventeen with Samuel de Champlain. He suffered through that winter at Quebec City, where scurvy and dysentery took the lives of twenty out of twenty-nine men. In 1610 he accompanied Champlain to an Indian rendezvous at the junction of the St. Lawrence and Richelieu rivers, where he met a group of Algonkins. With Champlain's blessing, Brûlé stayed to live among the Algonkin to learn their language and way of life. Brûlé spent much of his life with the Indians, eventually becoming unpopular with both the English and French because of his lack of allegiance to either side in their struggle for control of the fur trade. He was killed in 1632, allegedly by Hurons who ritually boiled and ate him.

During the summer of 1611, Champlain camped near the St. Louis rapids on the St. Lawrence River (the site of present-day Montreal), where he had previously arranged to meet with a group of Huron Indians. The Algonkin, who were trading partners with the Huron, had heard of Champlain's visit and paddled down the Ottawa to meet him. When the Algonkin left, Champlain sent a young man named Nicolas de Vignau with them, giving him a detailed memorandum of things that he ought to observe while with the tribe.

When Vignau returned to France in 1612, he reported, to Champlain's delight, that he had seen the Northern Sea (Hudson Bay), the key to the supposed trade route to the east. A lake, he claimed, at the head of the Ottawa flowed into it and could be reached in seventeen days by canoe from the St. Louis rapids.

In the spring of 1613, Champlain, with Vignau, three other Frenchmen and a "savage" set out in search of this Northern Sea. They travelled up the Ottawa River, hauled their canoes and supplies around the spectacular Chaudière Falls and paddled past the Eardley Escarpment and the lookout that now bears Champlain's name. It was not until they had reached an Algonkin settlement on Morrison Island in Allumette Lake, ninety kilometres west of Ottawa, that Vignau confessed that his stories of the Northern Sea had been false and that he had never been farther up river than this village. Although unsuccessful in its intended purpose, the journey did allow Champlain to map new territories and expand the fur trade empire of the French. The Ottawa River soon became a major access route for explorers and traders travelling westward through Lake Nipissing to the Great Lakes.

HURLING DOWN THE PINE

Almost two centuries after Brûlé and Champlain explored the region, settlers began to make their way up the Ottawa River. In 1796 an American named Philemon Wright came to the area looking for a place to settle and establish a community. Wright returned four years later accompanied by his family, five other families and some single labourers from Woburn, Massachusetts. Their caravan of seven horse- and ox-drawn sleighs travelled up the frozen Ottawa River, arriving at the mouth of the Gatineau on March 7, 1800. They immediately set to work clearing the land and building homes on the west bank of the Gatineau. The community they founded became known as Wrightsville, now the City of Hull.

Philemon Wright's first raft of squared timber on its way down the Ottawa River to Quebec City in 1806.

Wright and his companions had come with the intention of farming. However, their attention soon turned to the forest. In 1803 Britain was preparing for war with France and desperately needed timber to build ships for the Royal Navy. Their own resources exhausted, and the ports of Europe cut off by the French, Britain's attention turned to North America and the pines of the Ottawa Valley. The first load of squared timber and boards was floated down the Ottawa River from Wrightsville to Quebec City in 1806. Soon, the timber industry was flourishing and the Gatineau forests echoed with the ringing of axes and the crash of falling trees.

Lumbermen of the day headed into the woods as the leaves were changing in late September and did not return to their families until spring. Throughout the long winter, they lived in camps called "shanties" deep in the forest. Anywhere from thirty to a hundred and twenty men lived in each shanty, packed like sardines into one-room log cabins. In a typical cabin, forty men slept on bunks surrounding a huge fire pit. Above the fire, a large hole in the ceiling served as a chimney, ensuring that the air was always fresh, if not a little crisp.

Life in the shanties was hard. The men were up before dawn and worked until dark six days a week, cutting down the pines and hauling them by horse or oxen to the edge of a river. In spring, as soon as the ice went out and water levels were at their highest, the logs were floated down river to the mills. This camp song from the 1840s is reminiscent of the hard work and camaraderie among the shantymen.

The first year in the bush.

The Lumber Camp Song

Come all you jolly fellows and listen to my song;
It's all about the shanty boys and how they get along.
We're the jolliest bunch of fellows that ever you could find;
The way we spend our winter months is hurling down the pine.

At four o'clock each morning the boss begins to shout:
"Heave out, my jolly teamsters; it's time to start the route."
The teamsters they will all jump up in a most fretful way:
"Where is me boots? Where is me pants? Me socks is gone astray!"

At six o'clock it's breakfast, and ev'ry man is out,
For ev'ry man who is not sick will sure be on the route,
There's sawyers and there's choppers for to lay the timber low;
There's swampers and there's loggers to drag it to and fro.

And then comes up the logger, all at the break of day:
"Load up my slide, five hundred feet; to the river drive away."
You can hear those axes ringing until the sun goes down.
"Hurrah, my boys! The day is spent. To the shanty we are bound."

And when we reach the shanty, with cold hands and wet feet,
We there pull off our larrigans, our supper for to eat.
We sing and dance till nine o'clock; then to our bunks we climb.
Those winter months they won't be long in hurling down the pine.

The springtime rolls around at last, and then the boss will say:
"Heave down your saws and axes, boys, and help to clear away."
And when the floating ice goes out, in business we will thrive:
Two hundred able-bodied men are wanted on the drive.[1]

Shanty on the Black River.

In the early years of the timber trade, the shanty-men's diet consisted almost entirely of peas with pork and fresh-baked bread. Sundays provided time to catch a few fresh fish, and occasionally the cook might prepare some raisin pie — a much savoured delight.

Supplying the shanties became an industry in itself. Each year hundreds of barrels of flour, pork and peas, blankets, tools and other equipment, as well as the thousands of pounds of hay required to feed the draught animals, had to be hauled up the frozen Gatineau River by horse-drawn sleigh.

Stopping places, where a driver and his team could find food and shelter for the night, were established along the river. Originally a ramshackle collection of bunk houses and crude stables, these depots provided a catalyst for the development of communities such as Wakefield, Low, Kazabazua and Gracefield when settlers began to follow the lumbermen up the Gatineau in the 1830s.

Lumbermen in a shanty.

EARLY SETTLERS IN GATINEAU PARK

Asa Meech

The first settlers around Gatineau Park were Americans who arrived on the heels of Philemon Wright and his companions. The majority established small farms across the Gatineau River at Point Gatineau and west of Wrightsville toward Aylmer. A few families, however, made their way up the Gatineau River as far as the first major rapids. In a broad, fertile valley west of the river, they established the community of Chelsea (now Old Chelsea), named after its New England counterpart, Chelsea, Vermont.

One of Old Chelsea's founding and most distinguished members was the Reverend Asa Meech, who moved from his home in Charlotte, Vermont, to Wrightsville during the winter of 1815, where he preached at St. James Anglican Church. In 1821 he became the first to settle near the lake that now bears his name, when he was granted 200 acres of land bordering its east end. Asa was a man of many talents. He served as minister and doctor for the community in Old Chelsea and taught both Sunday school and regular school, all the while helping his wife raise a family and operate the farm.

Family life was not without its tragedies for Asa. His first wife, Mary DeWitt, died in 1809, leaving him with six young children, four of whom soon died either from illness or accident. Two years after Mary's death, Asa married her sister Maria. Together they had five children before tragedy struck again. In the spring of 1822, Maria and her three youngest children drowned in the flood waters of Brewery Creek. Legend has it that Asa's thick crop of hair turned completely

During the mid-1800s, immigrants, enticed from their homelands by the promise of free land, erected crude one-room log cabins throughout the forest around Meech Lake. To survive, many relied heavily on wild game, which they cooked in three-cornered iron pots on open fires in the centre of their dwellings, often with only a hole in the roof to serve as a chimney.

Hauling timber to the mill.

white that night. Asa went on to marry Margaret Docksteader and, with a little help from Margaret, "Old" Asa fathered another ten children before his death at the age of seventy-four in 1849.

Their son John maintained the family farm until his death in 1901. Built in 1821, the original Meech house — located on the south side of Meech Lake Road, four hundred metres east of the O'Brien Beach parking lot — is the oldest surviving structure in Gatineau Park. It is currently privately leased from the National Capital Commission.

Asa Meech is buried in the Protestant Burying Ground south of Chelsea Road in the heart of Old Chelsea. This burying ground is a rare example of an eighteenth-century New England cemetery. Unlike the manicured cemeteries of today, early New England burying grounds were dreary, unkept places — a reminder to all of their mortality and the torment that may await them in the grave. Tombstones were simple; many were probably made of wood and have long since disintegrated, leaving only humps and hollows to suggest that the ground was once turned over.

During the mid-1800s a number of English, Irish and Scottish families, enticed from their homelands by the promise of free land, made their homes "up the mountain" in the hills around Meech Lake. The land, as it turned out, came at the price of back-wrenching toil. The settlers laboured hard to clear the land of stones and stumps before planting wheat, oats, potatoes, peas and corn. Despite their heroic efforts, the rocky soil yielded crops reluctantly. In order to survive, many worked in sawmills on Meech and Harrington lakes and harvested fish from the lakes and game from the forest to get through the long winters.

Eventually they abandoned the farms, but if you look carefully among the hills around Meech Lake and along the Ridge Road, you can find piles of stones and old cedar fence rails that still outline cleared fields long since reclaimed by the forest.

In a trail guide written for the Ottawa Ski club in 1943, Charles Mortureaux described those who settled around Ridge Road this way:

> A small colony of Irish Families, sixteen in all, freshly arrived from the "old sod" settled in these hills, and cheerfully set to the task of clearing land that should never have been cleared and removing stones that should never have been removed because they made up practically nine tenths of the soil and kept cropping out as fast as they were piled up. The new settlers did not stay very many years, and probably would never have stayed at all had they not been light hearted sons and daughters of Ireland. It is said they made a fair brand of Irish whisky with the potatoes grown on this yellow soil, and very good gin with the juniper berries harvested in the mountain, and that may have been one of the reasons why they were loth to leave these remote hills. They grew tired, however, of scratching the barren soil; one by one they vacated their little clearings, their log shacks and the mountain, and the bush regained possession of their farms and of the road.[2]

The heritage of these early settlers lives on through the names of Paddy McCloskey, Garret Fortune and John Keogan — names that now identify ski trails and lodges within Gatineau Park.

John Harrington, after whom Harrington Lake is named, was the eldest son of a family that settled along the Mountain Road below Kingsmere Lake. He married one of Asa Meech's daughters and built the first house on the shore of Meech Lake. Harrington Lake is also commonly known as Lac Mousseau after the Mousseau family who settled nearby.

THE VILLAGE OF WAKEFIELD: "UP THE GATINEAU!"

While one group of hardy pioneers were scratching a living from the hills around Meech Lake, others were planting their hopes and dreams on the banks of the Gatineau River. Some of the earliest of these settled at the present site of Wakefield along the northeast border of Gatineau Park, at the junction of the Gatineau and Pêche rivers.

The Village of Wakefield, known in its early years as "The Pêche" was unofficially founded by a young Irish immigrant couple, Mary and Joseph Irwin. Joseph came to Canada to work at Bytown at the age of nineteen. He was joined soon after by his wife and their young son James. In the summer of 1829, the three of them loaded their belongings into a canoe and paddled and portaged their way into the wilderness that lay up the Gatineau River. That summer they built their first home on the southwest bank at the junction of the Gatineau and Pêche rivers, just in time for the birth of their second child.

The Irwins were soon followed by other families escaping hard times in the British Isles. Within a few years, dozens of small farms were scattered along the banks of the Gatineau River. Among these newcomers was a millwright from Roxburghshire, Scotland, named William Fairbairn. Fairbairn, like Joseph Irwin, worked for a time in Bytown, building locks on the Rideau Canal, before moving up the Gatineau to establish a homestead just north of the Pêche River opposite the Irwins' property.

The growing community of farmers was in need of a local mill to grind their grain, and Fairbairn set to the task of providing one. He purchased mill stones and gearings and petitioned the Governor of Upper and Lower Canada for permission to build a gristmill, stating that the region where he was settled was "a place destitute of mills ... being distant twenty-four miles from a grist mill."[3] Permission was granted, and in 1838 Fairbairn built Wakefield's first gristmill on the south bank of the Pêche River, five hundred metres upstream from where it flows into the Gatineau.

The mill, however, did not remain in his hands for long. In 1840 another Scottish couple, David and Elizabeth Maclaren, left their oldest son to care for their farm in Richmond, Ontario, and moved the rest of their family to Wakefield, where they quickly began to make their presence felt. In 1844 their two sons John and James purchased William Fairbairn's mill. More than a little whisky is rumoured to have encouraged the sale. Beside the mill they built a sawmill, a woollen factory, a brick-making plant and houses for the mill workers.

The Maclarens' mill complex on the Pêche River at Wakefield, circa 1865.

The Maclarens' woollen mill, circa 1900.

On a hill overlooking the entire complex, David Maclaren built for his two sons a large red brick home, which became known as the bachelor house.

Maclaren's gristmill produced a dark, stone-ground wheat flour. When highly refined white flour became available, it was regarded with high esteem and considered a superior product. Although nutritionists may refute this today, the misconception led to a priceless incident described by A. B. Robb in her *History of Wakefield Village*, published in 1959. The Mr. Edmond referred to is John Edmond, who worked as miller for the Maclarens for more than forty years before his death in 1911.

One day, a farmer, who must remain anonymous — brought his wheat to the mill to be ground, just as Mr. Edmond was about to go to dinner. He explained to the farmer how to tend the machine, so the flour would not overflow the container, and left for his noon-day meal. The farmer, his grinding done, bagged his flour and also left for dinner.

Some time later he returned, complaining that his wife couldn't use the flour, "it got as hard as a stone when she added water to it." A little investigation by Mr. Edmond revealed that the customer, left alone, had slyly added to the brown flour some white substance from another barrel nearby, believing it to be some of the coveted new style flour, and that he could improve his mix at no cost to himself. Unfortunately for the schemer, the lovely white "flour" was not flour at all, but some plaster of paris which Mr. Edmond was using to repair the grinding stones.[4]

Maclaren's General Store, circa 1900.

In addition to the mill complex, the Maclaren family established Wakefield's first general store on the main street overlooking the Gatineau River. Maclaren's General Store began as a small log cabin in which the owners unrolled their blankets and slept at day's end. From these humble beginnings, the shop grew to become a two-and-a-half-story brick building with several outlying buildings, including a warehouse and a stable. In its heyday, the shop housed a millinery, a dressmaking salon, Wakefield's first post office, and a banking service that offered local residents three and a half percent interest on their savings, half a percentage higher than was customary in Wrightsville. Although oil lamps and candles were the standard source of lighting at the time, a private electric generator installed at the mill complex provided the general store with electric light years before it was available to the rest of the village. For almost a hundred years, Maclaren's General Store was a focal point in the community, where farmers traded fresh produce for dry goods such as fabric, sugar and flour or a badly needed new pair of boots. Once again, Ms. Robb describes a humorous incident at the store, which, in her words, provides "a bit of local color":

> A notable farm butter-maker brought in a tub of her famous butter for sale. Speaking very confidentially to the salesman, Jack McDonald by name, she confided a mouse had fallen into the cream to an untimely death.

"I couldn't bear to throw out all that cream, but of course I couldn't use it. Couldn't you just exchange it for me? For what the eye don't see, the belly don't taste."

The courteous and understanding employe [*sic*] took the tub of butter, turned the butter into a different tub, and returned a different tub but the same butter to the lady, while repeating her own words, "What the eye doesn't see, the belly doesn't taste."[5]

The Maclarens' prosperity was tempered with its share of bad luck. Their sawmill burned down during the 1850s and the gristmill and woollen factory suffered the same fate in 1877. The family rebuilt all the buildings, only to have them destroyed again in 1910 by a devastating fire that spread to the surrounding hills and threatened to engulf the entire community before rain doused the flames the following day. This time the Maclarens rebuilt only the gristmill. In 1941 a faulty light bulb exploded in the oil room of Maclaren's General Store and that, too, was lost to fire.

In 1891 the Gatineau Valley Railway Company completed construction of a rail line from Hull to Wakefield. At a time when horse-drawn buggies vastly outnumbered automobiles on the rough dirt roads winding up the valley, the introduction of rail service had a tremendous impact. Both passengers and freight could be moved much more easily, and Wakefield soon became a popular recreational spot, with boarding houses and shops catering to tourists and cottagers escaping the hustle and bustle of the city. At its peak in the early part of this century, the line carried two trains in each direction every day except Sunday, as well as an express train for the cottager traffic on weekends. Here, as across the continent, improvements in automotive technology caused rail service to dwindle. The last passenger train rolled up the line in 1963 and the last freight train in 1968.

The Maclaren home, circa 1900.

Today, Wakefield retains strong ties with its past. Direct descendants of the original settlers still operate many farms in the region. Several nineteenth-century buildings have survived and are preserved as heritage sites, including Maclaren's gristmill and the red brick home overlooking the mill complex. Both have been converted to museums that offer a revealing glimpse at the early days of settlement around Gatineau Park.

Passenger rail service has been revived on the old Gatineau Valley Railway line with an authentic steam powered train that carries tourists between Hull and Wakefield throughout the summer months.

In 1915 one of the longest covered bridges in Quebec, the Gendron Bridge, was built across the Gatineau River at Wakefield. The bridge was destroyed by an arsonist in 1984, but as a testament to their enthusiasm for embracing the rich heritage of their village, local residents founded the Wakefield Covered Bridge Project. They have recruited volunteers and solicited donations from visitors and supplies from local businesses, and they expect to have the bridge rebuilt soon using traditional methods and materials.

THE OTTAWA SKI CLUB

Toward the end of the nineteenth century, the fresh air and clear lakes of the Gatineau Hills beckoned city dwellers northward, and summer homes and cottages began to spring up around the shores of Meech and Kingsmere lakes. In 1914 Andrew Alexander, son of early Meech Lake residents Mary and James Alexander, and his wife Emma opened a lakeside hotel called

Meach Lake House [sic]. The three cars in the photograph, sporting signs that say "Alexander's Cars to Meach Lake," were used to transport guests between the hotel and the train station at Chelsea.

Meach Lake House [*sic*]. From May to October, their hotel was busy with folk escaping the hustle and bustle of Ottawa and Hull to enjoy fishing, boating, tennis and hiking in the fresh country air. Around the same time, cross-country skiers began to explore the hills around Chelsea and Kingsmere. The Alexanders were themselves keen skiers, and Meach Lake House soon became a popular stopping spot where skiers could enjoy a fine meal. James made his family's skis himself, cutting the fittings from old leather drive belts salvaged from the sawmills.

In 1910 the Ottawa Ski Club was formed. The club was composed of two groups of skiers with some crossover between the disciplines. There were the "plank-hoppers" who concentrated their activities around the ski jump on Suicide Hill in Rockcliffe Park, and there were the over-land skiers, or "cake eaters" as they were known to the jumpers. The cake eaters held their first official cross-country race in 1914 from Murphy's Inn at Kingsmere, via Pink and Fairy lakes, to Rockcliffe. In 1920 the Ottawa Ski Club purchased a small woodcutter's shack in the Gatineau Hills and opened their first lodge, which they named Camp Fortune after its original owner.

By this time there was an extensive network of trails connecting Hull to communities on the Gatineau River, including Chelsea Station, Tenaga, Kirks Ferry and Cascades. Sunday mornings the northbound train from Union Station in Ottawa was crowded with people, skis and piles of winter clothing. Some got off at Chelsea Station to ski up to Kingsmere and then back to Hull, but most continued on to Tenaga, Kirks Ferry, Burnet or Cascades. From Cascades they could ski to Meach Lake House for a hearty noon meal, before moving on to Camp Fortune and then to Hull via Pink and Fairy lakes. This was roughly a thirty-two-kilometre trip and, considering the heavy wooden skis used at the time, must have been a good day's exercise.

The atmosphere of early ski outings in Gatineau Park is reflected by the following article, written by Luke McLuke and published in the club's newsletter *Ottawa Ski Club News*, February 23, 1927. At the time, women skiers had only recently exchanged their cumbersome skirts for trousers, and McLuke points out that not everyone approved of the new fashion.

Skiers beside the woodcutter's shack that was purchased by the Ottawa Ski Club in 1920 and converted into the first Camp Fortune Lodge.

Skiers leaving the train at Kirks Ferry to take the trail to Camp Fortune or Murphy's Inn at Kingsmere.

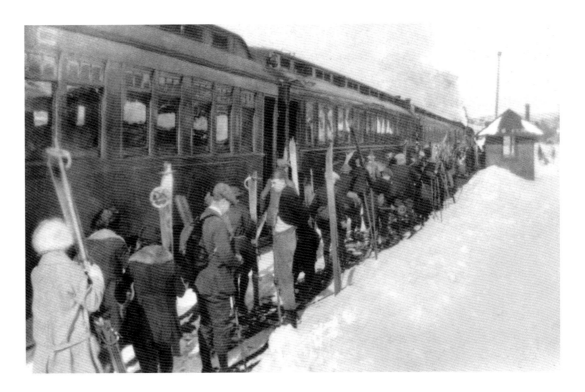

THE SENSATIONS OF A SUNDAY SKIER

BY LUKE McLUKE

Dawn, the rosy-fingered. The springing lightly from the couch. The dash to the verandah to verify the satisfactory sub-zero mark of the mercury. The mad assembling of neglected necessities. The bolted breakfast. The rotten car service. The Central Station with its punctual impatient skiers and their procrastinating respective skeeties. The Ski Special with its forest-like vistas of skis and poles. The departure and the inevitable last man dashing through the concourse to flatten his nose against the closed gate.

The smell of smoke and orange peelings. The profiteering news-butcher. The women and children who leave the train at Ironsides and Chelsea. Kirk's Ferry where men are men and the women dress like them. The drag up McAllister's. The piffling hill down to Dunlop's. The tiresome trail through the brush. The enchanting odor of wood smoke on the frosty air. The last heartbreaking hill up to the Lodge.

The delicious odors of sausages, steak and onions and baked beans. The actual sight of food. The dearth of frying pans and tea pots. The hounding of the lucky possessor thereof. The actual taste of food. The surreptitious unbuckling of the belt. The inevitable loss of appetite. The gradual glazing of the eyes. The subsequent serpent-like state of coma. The sudden realization of the passage of time and the decision to move on. The disgusting spectacle of intelligent people deliberately over eating. The sickening smell of cooking food.

The open air, the tang of the frost and the crunching of the snow underfoot. The mad exhilaration of George's Hill. The sudden curve and the girl sprawling across the narrow trail waiting for sympathy. The mad stemming and snow-plowing and the successful swerve. The utter lack of sympathy, felt or expressed. The resultant dirty look.

The cold sweep of the wind across Kingsmere. The interesting curves and dips of the Mica Mine Trail. The cold austerity of the tyler at Pink Lake and Wetmore's cheerful smile as an antidote. The reviving second pot of tea. The flash of yellow representing Birch Valley Lodge, *en passant*. The Hill and Dale. The long drag across the open into Wrightville [*sic*]. The final, definite decision to give up ski-ing.

The helpful but not entirely disinterested kids at the Wrightville terminus. The remarks of the Early Victorian Lady on the car: "A lot of bold hussies gallivanting around on a Sunday in men's pants." The cold and clammy waiting at transfer points. The confirmation of the decision concerning giving up ski-ing. Home.

The generous jolt of Jamaica. The tingling at the tips of the toes. The changed outlook on life in general and the reconsideration of the decision regarding giving up ski-ing. The hot bath — chin deep. The old dressing gown and the slippers. The smell of cooking. The changed attitude toward food and eating it. The plans for next Sunday. The Ostermoor. The arms of Morpheus.[6]

As skiing increased in popularity, the club's Night Riders, an enthusiastic band of volunteers who served as route finders, brush clearers and first aiders, developed the extensive network of trails around Camp Fortune that includes Highland, Pleasant Valley and the Merry-Go-Round, among others.

In 1921 a lodge opened at Pink Lake that became a popular stopping spot between Camp Fortune and Hull. In 1923 the rival Cliffside Ski Club erected the first lodge in Keogan's clearing. The East Side Lodge opened in 1925 opposite Tenaga on the east side of the Gatineau River. Little used, it was dismantled in 1930 and its materials were incorporated into Western Lodge on the edge of the escarpment. In an article in the *Ottawa Ski Club News* of December 24, 1930, club president Charles Mortureaux described the new lodge.

> Somewhere along the ridge, however, three miles west of Camp Fortune as the crow flies ... a new lodge has arisen, not in the shadow of a barn as her poor sister of the East was, but on the top of a cliff, rising perpendicularly 500 feet above the level fields below, and from which the whole of the Ottawa Valley can be seen in its wintry splendour, as far as Arnprior — a magnificent look-out, the best perhaps of all those that have been discovered in the whole Gatineau country.[7]

Downhill skiing was introduced to the Gatineau Hills in 1932 when the Joe Morin Slalom Hill opened in the Camp Fortune valley. The first rope tow was powered by an old Cadillac engine, dragged across the snow to the hill during the winter of 1939-40. As downhill skiing became increasingly popular, more hills were cleared and a large alpine resort developed at Camp Fortune. Cross-country ski touring soon slipped from the limelight and both Western and the Pink Lake lodges were dismantled. During the late 1950s, a cabin that had been dismantled to make way for construction of the Gatineau Parkway was rebuilt on the site of Western Lodge.

Herridge Lodge, nestled deep in the forest north of Harrington Lake, was originally the home of the Cafferty family, who operated a small farm on the site from about 1880 to 1906. William Herridge, a former Canadian Ambassador to the United States, used it as a winter retreat for over forty years before its acquisition by the National Capital Commission.

Today Gatineau Park contains almost two hundred kilometres of groomed trails boasting some of the best cross-country skiing in eastern Canada. Each winter the park hosts the Gatineau 55, one of eleven world loppet ski races, attracting enthusiastic skiers from North America and Europe, including some of the world's fastest racers. For those who prefer a lift on the uphill sections, there are now two alpine resorts, Camp Fortune and Vorlage. For the adventurous skier or snowshoer, the remote western portion of the park beckons with expanses of untracked forest and beaver swamps where one can wander for days.

THOMAS "CARBIDE" WILLSON

Thomas "Carbide" Willson

Hidden among the hills at the north end of Little Meech Lake stand the ruins of an old dam and powerhouse known locally as "The Mill." Popular as a destination for skiers, hikers and sunbathers, these mysterious structures were built by one of Meech Lake's most industrious residents, Thomas "Carbide" Willson.

Thomas Leopold Willson was an electro-chemist and a remarkable inventor and entrepreneur. Among his many achievements was the discovery of a relatively inexpensive process for producing calcium carbide by heating lime and coke in an electric furnace. In the days before batteries, carbide lamps provided a safe, efficient and portable light by burning the acetylene gas produced by the reaction between calcium carbide crystals and water. They were used extensively as miners' lamps and as headlamps on buggies and early automobiles and are still used today by many spelunkers. Willson's discovery was a tremendous breakthrough; soon he held patents in over forty countries and controlled sales through an international syndicate. His lamps lighted the railcars of the Canadian Pacific Railway and the shipping lanes of the St. Lawrence River.

In 1907 the Willson family built a magnificent summer home at the top of a cliff overlooking the southeast end of Meech Lake. The house had eleven bedrooms, and, despite seven fireplaces, it took two wood-burning furnaces to heat the place. To ensure he was not cut off from important business communications, Willson installed a private telephone line all the way from Old Chelsea. Despite

the beauty of the surrounding hills, Mrs. Willson longed for a flower garden. The ground around the house was too rocky and exposed, but in the woods nearby, a small stream trickled through a valley, sheltered on one side by a hill and on the other by a stunning pink granitic cliff. Willson dammed the stream, creating a private pond and flower garden, hidden from prying eyes by the forest. (Photograph on page 103.)

Over the years, Thomas Willson began to focus his attention on the scientific investigation of nitrogen. In the basement of his Ottawa home, he installed a well equipped nitrogen-research laboratory, and his investigations soon led to the development of a revolutionary new phosphate fertilizer. In the laboratory, however, he could produce only a few pounds of fertilizer each day. To test the commercial potential of his discovery, he needed a plant that could produce fertilizer by the ton. The waterfall where Little Meech Lake overflows into Meech Creek was the perfect site, and there he built the world's first phosphoric acid condensation plant. In 1911 he began construction on the dam, creating havoc for the other residents of Meech Lake. Water levels in the lake fluctuated from day to day, leaving boathouses alternately six feet under and then six feet above the water line! Construction was completed on the dam, a powerhouse and an acid condensation tower in 1913. One can easily imagine the site on a stormy night — flashes of lightning, driving rain and gusts of wind providing the perfect backdrop for the humming of generators and the neon blue flashes of light emanating from within the powerhouse.

The experiment was a success. Convinced that he was on the verge of creating a new industrial empire, Willson sold his many companies and mortgaged all his

Thomas Willson's powerhouse and acid condensation tower under construction, circa 1913.

rights, patents and properties. Misfortune followed. When Willson did not meet his production deadlines, all of his assets were seized. Given time, Thomas Willson no doubt would have bounced back and brought his dream of a new empire to fruition. Instead, he died of heart failure in New York in 1915 while he was trying to raise the necessary capital.

Neglected, the acid condensation tower on Meech Creek burned down and the dam and powerhouse fell into disrepair. Today only skeletons of the original structures remain. You can visit them by following a wooded trail that begins at the O'Brien Beach parking lot at the southeast end of Meech Lake. As you walk along the shore of Little Meech Lake, be on the lookout for the muskrats that frequent the water's edge.

The beautiful Willson home is easily visible on the cliff above Meech Lake. It is maintained by the National Capital Commission and serves as a federal government conference centre. This is where the famous Meech Lake Accord, the failed constitutional amendment of 1990, was hammered out. Mrs. Willson's flower garden has been reclaimed by the forest but the pond still lies hidden among the trees, home to a family of beavers and a "secret" swimming hole for generations of adventurous young explorers.

THE MACKENZIE KING ESTATE

I hereby bequeath to the Government of Canada as a public park in trust for the citizens of Canada ... my several properties at Kingsmere, in the province of Quebec, amounting in all to nearly five hundred acres, and the houses and other buildings erected thereon ... I express the wish that the lands at Kingsmere may be maintained as nearly as possible in their present state; that they will be developed as parkland, and that they will form a wildlife sanctuary and will continue to have the character of a natural forest reserve.[8]

FROM THE LAST WILL AND TESTAMENT OF THE
RIGHT HONOURABLE WILLIAM LYON MACKENZIE KING.

Mackenzie King hiking in the woods near Kingsmere.

For fifty years William Lyon Mackenzie King made his summer home in the Gatineau Hills at Kingsmere. During that time he developed an estate that included two summer homes, two cottages, an extensive array of farmlands, gardens and woodland trails, and an extraordinary collection of ruins.

Mackenzie King's passion for the Gatineau Hills began on Thanksgiving Day in 1900 when he and a friend cycled along the dusty gravel roads from Ottawa to Kingsmere. The following summer he took up residence at Mrs. McMinn's boarding-house in Kingsmere, commuting by train to his job with the Ministry of Labour in Ottawa.

In 1903 King purchased a hectare of land on the south side of Kingsmere Lake and erected a modest four-room cottage, which he called Kingswood.

Mackenzie King relaxing at Kingswood.

Swimming at the Kingswood boathouse, Kingsmere Lake, circa 1917.

King expanded Kingswood and built a boathouse to accommodate a canoe and to provide a proper place for ladies to change for swimming or to have a "lake bath" in privacy. He then purchased a neighbouring cottage as a guest house for visitors.

In 1923 King acquired Edgmoor, a small cottage on the hilltop, a short distance from the lake. He changed the name of the cottage to Moorside and began an ambitious series of renovations that transformed the one-and-a-half-story building into a sprawling country home with modern plumbing and electricity. Moorside was King's summer home from 1929 to 1939 and the centrepiece of the estate around which he designed the extensive lawns and manicured gardens. As prime minister from 1926 to 1930 and from 1935 to 1948, King entertained Winston Churchill and other world leaders at Moorside.

One day in 1935, King drove by a house being demolished on Daly Avenue in Ottawa. At one end of the site stood a large stone bay window frame that had not yet been torn down. Inspired by the statues and ruins in European and English gardens, King had, for a number of years, been looking for suitable ruins to erect on his Moorside property. After some negotiation with the contractor, he purchased the bay window for $50 and paid an additional $200 for transportation and reassembly at Kingsmere. "The Abbey" so delighted King that he salvaged more stone from the Daly Avenue house and had a second ruin, a corner wall containing a window and doorway, installed at the same site. Between 1935 and 1937, King installed a number of other ruins on the grounds around Moorside. He salvaged pillars from the British North American Bank Note Company in Ottawa to construct the "Window on the Forest" in the Moorside gardens and the "Arc de Triomphe," which stands enshrouded by forest in the area King called "Diana's Grove." Two additional walls were added to "The Abbey" from stone and a fireplace King collected from the burned debris of the original Parliament Buildings. King justified the construction of the ruins as a way of creating a lasting legacy to his name, as well as a means of preserving Canada's heritage.

Among the many properties engulfed by the expanding estate was "The Farm." King had a romantic, idealized view of farming life and was more excited by the pastoral splendour of his sheep in the fields than he was with its practical operation. Although his farm never made a profit, he maintained it as a hobby throughout his lifetime. The original farmhouse was extensively renovated and winterized and eventually became King's home. It was here that he died in 1950.

Today, visitors to the Mackenzie King Estate may walk among the ruins and flower gardens or follow King's favourite woodland trail to Bridal Veil Falls. Moorside houses a Mackenzie King museum and a cosy tearoom open to the public during the summer months. The Farm serves as the Official Residence of the Speaker of the House of Commons and is not open to the public.

THE POLITICS OF CONSERVATION

The notion of creating a national park in the Gatineau Hills dates back to the turn of the century. In 1899 Prime Minister Sir Wilfrid Laurier, inspired by the beauty of the American capital and anxious to build a "Washington of the North," created the Ottawa Improvement Commission. The Commission was given a mandate to beautify the capital and empowered by Parliament to buy land for the development of public parks and scenic boulevards. In his city plan report, tabled for the Commission in 1903, landscape architect Frederick Todd first proposed the establishment of a large nature preserve near the capital in the Gatineau Hills. Todd argued that Canada was famous for its forests and that it was therefore appropriate to set aside an example of original Canadian forest lands near the capital for future generations. His recommendation, however, was opposed and even ridiculed by some Commission members. Despite strong reaffirmation of Todd's recommendation in the Holt Commission plan for the capital in 1913, no action was taken for more than thirty years.

Many people championed the creation of a national park in the Gatineau Hills, but few were ultimately more influential than William Lyon Mackenzie King. During the Great Depression of the 1930s, much of the park's hardwood forests were being cut down for fuelwood. Land owners sold timber stands to wood dealers who paid labourers a dollar a day to clearcut the land. As early as the late 1920s King had decided to bequeath his estate at Kingsmere to the people of Canada as a national park, and he was gravely concerned about the indiscriminate cutting of the forest around his summer home.

Construction of the Gatineau Parkway north of Old Chelsea.

Stonemasons building the Étienne Brûlé Lookout on the Champlain Parkway, September 1956.

On May 23, 1935, King gave an impassioned speech in the House of Commons in which he pleaded for the preservation of the Gatineau Hills.

> I think hon. members would be horrified if they could see what has happened within the last two years within a radius of ten or fifteen miles of the City of Ottawa. Whole hillsides which face the approaches to Ottawa from other parts of the country have been completely denuded of their trees. There have been left devastated areas which are nothing else but barren rocks and eroded soil.... Streams and springs are drying up, and the wild life of woods and waters disappearing.[9]

King also introduced a parliamentary bill that replaced the Ottawa Improvement Commission with the Federal District Commission and broadened its mandate to include beautification planning on both sides of the Ottawa River. He was then able to encourage the appropriation of money for the Commission to purchase land for the creation of a national park.

Outside Parliament a grassroots movement to preserve the Gatineau Hills was developing. The Ottawa Ski Club organized a campaign to purchase land around their ski trails. Club members, along with other concerned citizens, including R. B. Bennett, Sir Robert Borden and Governor General Bessborough, formed the Federal Woodlands Preservation League to fight the indiscriminate cutting of trees on privately owned land in the Gatineau Hills. In 1936 a proposal to build a scenic parkway connecting the capital with the Gatineau Hills was widely debated. Prominent politicians praised the scheme both as an enrichment of the capital area and, equally important, as an unemployment relief program. In 1938, under mounting public pressure, a resolution was passed in the House of Commons to acquire land in the Gatineau Hills. By 1939 the Federal District Commission had acquired six and a half hectares and begun clearing trails and building scenic lookouts; however, the outbreak of war in Europe put development of the park on hold until 1945.

While in Paris in 1936, Mackenzie King met French city planner Jacques Gréber. King was impressed with Gréber's ideas and invited him to Canada the following year to help develop a new city plan for the Capital. Gréber returned to France during the war but, at King's request, returned in 1945 to oversee the development of a long-term master plan for the National Capital Region. Jacques Gréber recommended the creation of a green belt around the city, completion of the parkway in the Gatineau Hills, and expansion of Gatineau Park to a total of 33,600 hectares. Persistent lobbying eventually bore fruit, and the Gréber Plan was passed in the House of Commons in 1951. Since then, acquisition of park lands has been a slow process that continues today. In 1991 an ailing Camp Fortune was purchased from the Ottawa Ski Club, significantly reducing the amount of privately owned land within the park. Today, only about 1,000 of the park's 35,700 hectares are still private lands.

Although it was set aside as a "national" park for the benefit of all Canadians, Gatineau Park does not have national park status. It is maintained and administered by the National Capital Commission, the most recent incarnation of the Ottawa Improvement Commission and the Federal District Commission. To the Commission's credit, Gatineau Park is probably closer to its natural state today than it has been throughout much of this century. There are fewer homes in the park now than there were during the 1950s, and deer, beaver and other wildlife populations are healthy. Despite this, as highways and housing developments encroach on the park and as pressure for developing public recreational facilities mounts, the park's fragile wilderness character is threatened.

Gatineau Park exists because a previous generation cared deeply enough to fight for its protection. Perhaps the greatest challenge facing those of us who care about Gatineau Park today is seeing that it does not suffer from overuse, or become merely an island of green in a sea of urban development. As the surrounding human population increases, more land needs to be set aside for recreational use, wildlife habitats must be preserved, and corridors of green must be maintained to allow wildlife to migrate in and out of the park. Only through active participation, be it dialogue with the National Capital Commission, supporting local conservation groups, or lobbying industry and politicians at all levels of government, can we ensure a healthy future for Gatineau Park. Ultimately we are all stewards of Gatineau Park and of Earth.

THE PHOTOGRAPHS

Dead trees in a valley near Hay Lake.

The stream that flows out of Hay Lake is typical of many that drain the western portion of Gatineau Park. It flows through a valley where numerous beaver dams slow its progress to a trickle. Periodically, heavy rains cause the water level to rise, or a new dam diverts its flow, and a portion of the surrounding forest becomes submerged. The forest in this photograph was temporarily submerged, but the water did not drain soon enough for the trees to recover, so now only a ghostly skeleton of the forest remains.

Meadow and stream near Fortune Lake.

This valley was also once covered by a forest that was flooded by beavers. Eventually the beaver dam broke and the pond drained, revealing stumps of the old forest and creating a meadow that now provides habitat for songbirds and forage for deer, bears and other animals.

Canada anemone, blue flag iris and mosquito.

For a few days each spring, the showy petals of the beautiful blue flag iris grace low-lying portions of this field, where the ground is still moist from meltwater and rain. The anemone blossoms emerge at roughly the same time, but will continue to bloom long after the iris has withered away. I searched for some time before I found these flowers growing close together and then took several more minutes to carefully frame the composition. The mosquito arrived by chance, just as I was ready to trip the shutter, and was gone within seconds.

Canada anemone and buttercups.

In the same field in early summer, buttercups dwarf the Canada anemone, their long stems stretching toward the sun. Soon the anemone blossoms will be gone, replaced by daisies, clover, cow vetch and other summer flowers.

Reindeer lichen and blueberry leaves.

When I came upon this patch of blueberry leaves and reindeer lichen, I was immediately struck by its similarity to the vegetation that grows in the boreal forest in northern Canada. By excluding the surrounding flora, which would have provided a southern context, I created a photograph that reflects my initial impression. I have since used this photograph to lead off slide presentations of trips to the Northwest Territories and found that it evokes a similar response in others, immediately conjuring up memories of summers spent in the far north.

Mist enshrouded maple forest.

Sugar maple, the dominant tree species throughout much of Gatineau Park, is a climax species, meaning it grows in mature forests that regenerate themselves. Maple seedlings thrive in the shade of their predecessors, eventually taking their place and providing a well shaded, healthy environment for their own seedlings. This forest will reproduce itself indefinitely until outside influences such as climatic change or insect infestation alter its cycle. A green hue permeates this image — the result of light, bouncing off the maples' foliage, being diffused and reflected by millions of tiny water droplets suspended in the air.

Late summer frost in a valley near Pink Lake.

In September I anxiously await the first frosts, often rising before dawn to wander into the woods in search of photographs. Weeks before frost appears in the city, small pockets of moisture-laden air settle into valleys in the Gatineau Hills, leaving a thin covering of ice crystals that enhances the wonderful tapestry of autumn colours.

Wild strawberry leaves in an old field beside Notch Road.

Half buried beneath a matt of dry grass and flower stems, the tiny white blossoms of wild strawberries are among the first flowers to appear in old fields in spring. Although wild strawberries are much smaller than the familiar domestic variety, they are also much tastier and are a common food for a variety of birds and mammals, including black bears and raccoons.

BEAVER

In the nineteenth century, beaver pelt hats were very popular in North America and Europe. To quench the thirst for skins, trappers hunted the beaver almost to extinction throughout the Gatineau region. However, nine pairs of beavers, reintroduced during the mid-1940s, have since proliferated to one of the densest beaver populations in the world.

An estimated two thousand beavers now live in Gatineau Park and their effect on the park ecosystem is enormous. Beavers are the lumberjacks and the master builders of the forest community. In response to an instinctive urge, they pile up tree branches, reinforced with mud and debris, to construct dams wherever they encounter flowing water. Nearly every stream in Gatineau Park, even the tiniest trickle, has been dammed and redammed from its source to the park boundary, creating hundreds of small ponds and marshes that provide habitat for painted turtles, bullfrogs, muskrats, river otters, great blue herons, black ducks and a tremendous variety of other wildlife. Occasionally a family of beavers is killed off by predators, in which case their dam falls into disrepair and eventually breaks down, causing the pond to drain and creating a meadow that provides rich forage for deer, bears and other animals.

In addition to dams, beavers build lodges by stacking and interweaving tree branches, mud and debris into mounds. From beneath the water's surface, they tunnel into the mound and carve out a living chamber, leaving a thick covering of sticks and muck that freezes in winter. The result is a hard, igloo-like structure that provides shelter from the cold and is virtually impenetrable to predators. The standard model lodge extends about one metre above the water's surface and is equipped with one living chamber and two access tunnels; however, as succeeding generations add material and excavate new rooms, a lodge may grow to several times its original size. A portion of the lodge roof, left without mud reinforcement, serves as a chimney that allows air to circulate throughout the dwelling. On cold winter days, steam and currents of warm air can often be seen escaping through these "smoke holes" from beaver lodges throughout Gatineau Park.

Beavers mate in midwinter, with two or three kits arriving in spring or early summer. At birth they already have a thick coat of fur and can walk within minutes and swim within hours. Although they are weaned within about thirty days, the kits do not generally leave the lodge until they are two months old, and then they remain with their parents for two years, contributing to the building and maintenance of the lodge and dam.

During summer, beavers feed on aquatic plants such as water-lilies and pondweeds, often eating the entire plant — roots, stems, leaves and even flowers. Throughout the rest of the year, they eat the tender bark of saplings or young branches from the tops of felled trees, particularly aspen and birch. In autumn, they cache small branches in

piles, stuck into the mud on the bottom of the pond, which serve as a storehouse of food when the pond freezes over in winter.

Beavers are slow and vulnerable to predators while on land, but extremely well adapted to life in the water. When they dive, their heart rate drops to conserve oxygen; transparent eyelids allow them to see underwater; a waterproof valve system keeps water out of their ears and nose; and their hind feet are large and webbed, more like those of a duck than a rodent. When startled, a beaver may slap its broad tail against the water's surface as it dives — a warning to other family members that danger may be imminent.

Although any noise or sudden movement close to the water's edge is likely to disturb them, beavers are often quite tolerant of observers who remain a comfortable distance away. Probably the best time to watch is in the late afternoon, when they emerge from their dens to feed and groom before an evening of maintenance work and play. I have spent many an enjoyable afternoon sitting by the side of a pond, watching beavers break up a thin sheet of ice that had formed the night before or shuffle branches back and forth across the pond, every so often swimming over to have a closer look at their curious visitor.

Farm at the base of the Eardley Escarpment near Luskville.

The cliffs of the Eardley Escarpment form an abrupt boundary between the fertile plain of the Ottawa River Valley and the rugged landscape of Gatineau Park. Eleven thousand years ago, these cliffs formed the northern shore of an ancient arm of the Atlantic known as the Champlain Sea. Sea birds nested on the escarpment face and beluga, bowhead and humpback whales swam offshore.

North end of Harrington Lake.

North of the Eardley Escarpment, a rocky plateau dotted with small lakes, streams and beaver ponds leads to a series of rolling hills that descend toward the line of lakes Philippe, Harrington and Meech. During late September and early October, thousands of visitors flock to the parkways and forest trails in Gatineau Park to marvel at the hardwood forests of sugar maple and beech as they reach their height of autumn splendour.

Oak, maple and beech leaves in ice.

As a young boy I remember well the joy of smashing through ice on the surface of puddles. On the October morning when I took this photograph, I was both horrified and amused to discover young boys doing the same thing to puddles like this one on Ridge Road. Soon after these leaves froze into place, the puddle beneath them dried up, leaving only a fragile sheet of ice suspended several inches above the forest floor.

Maple and beech leaves illuminated by the setting sun.

At first glance this photograph has a strange, almost surreal appearance. Leaves appear to float on top of one another and the play of light and shadow is unfamiliar. Once it has been made apparent, the cause of these effects is obvious. It had been raining for several days before the photograph was taken, and the leaves are several inches beneath the surface of a large puddle.

Shrub with vine on a granite outcrop.

Most of the photographs in this book were taken either when the sky was overcast, or very early or late in the day when sunlight was least intense. Bright sunshine creates strong contrasts between highlights and shadows, which are beyond the range that film can reproduce while still retaining detail. This inability of film to reproduce what our eyes see restricts the kind of photographs that can be made, but at the same time provides a challenge for photographers to harness the expressive potential of well defined shadows while incorporating them as compositional elements.

Ironwood shadows and juniper on the Eardley Escarpment.

Shadows can add drama and intrigue to a photograph, particularly when the object casting the shadow is outside the picture space. This photograph was taken later in the day than the one opposite. The sunlight is less intense, bathing the rock in a warm glow and creating a soft play of light and shadow that reveals the texture of the rock's surface.

Barred owl near the Mackenzie King Estate.

Gatineau Park's dense mixed forests are ideal habitat for the barred owl, which, despite its size, flies through the maze of trunks and branches with remarkable skill and grace. This owl is patiently watching the mouth of a burrow, probably that of a shrew, hidden among grass and leaves on the forest floor.

Feather imprint near Meech Lake.

An owl's primary flight feathers have a softer, more broken edge than those of most birds, a trait that reduces the vortex noise of air passing over the wings, allowing owls to fly noiselessly. Owls also have remarkably sensitive hearing, which allows them to pinpoint the exact location of voles and other prey moving about under snow.

Trilliums in the forest near Hickory Trail.

Each May, a magnificent display of trilliums carpets the forest floor throughout Gatineau Park. As they age, their bright white petals shift to a soft pink. Scattered among these flowers grow a few red trilliums and the occasional painted trillium with its dash of bright red at the base of each small, white petal. Each trillium relies on its three broad leaves to gather the sunlight necessary for photosynthesis. Consequently, if the flower is picked by an admiring passerby, the remains of the plant will be unable to produce food and will likely die. Even if an adequate reserve of nutrients remains within the rootstock for it to survive the season, the plant will not flower again for several years.

Heart-leaved asters and sugar maples.

Long before they shared their discovery with Europeans, native North Americans distilled maple syrup from the sap of sugar maples, using it to sweeten foods and to impart a maple-cured flavour to cooked meat. Today the entire world production of maple syrup comes from a band of hardwood forest stretching from southern Ontario east to Nova Scotia and south into the north-eastern United States. A staggering two thirds of total production comes from Quebec forests.

BLACK BEAR

If you spend a lot of time in Gatineau Park, you may occasionally see black bears foraging for food along hiking trails or around lakeshores. More often than not, however, it will be only the hind end that you see as the bear lumbers off into the woods. On one occasion, when I was jogging along Ridge Road, a mother and cub ran across the trail in front of me. A second cub, which was straggling a short distance behind, caught sight of me charging toward it and came to a dead stop in the middle of the trail. I dug in my heels to avoid running over the little fellow and, for a few seconds, we just stood and stared at each other in wide-eyed surprise. Out of the corner of my eye I could see the mother stop and turn in our direction, but she didn't seem too concerned. She waited patiently, and in a moment the cub regained its composure and hurried off into the woods, leaving me with a little grin on my face that lasted well into the night and probably a good portion of the next day.

Of all the bears, black bears are the most omnivorous, eating whatever animals they can catch. These include mice, shrews and voles, as well as insects such as beatles and ants, which they uncover by turning over rocks or tearing apart rotting logs. The bulk of their diet, however, is vegetarian. In spring, when they are at their hungriest and food is scarce, they eat the new shoots and buds of grasses, shrubs and trees. In fall, as delicacies such as nuts, berries and mushrooms become available, black bears feast almost non-stop, consuming hundreds of pounds of food to put on the layer of fat that will serve as their winter storehouse. Deep claw marks in the bark of many beech trees in the park are evidence that bears have climbed up searching for one of their favourite foods — the beech nut. Often they sit in the upper branches, breaking off nearby limbs and stripping them of nuts.

Occasionally these broken branches collect in "bear nests" — piles of branches that look like giant nests in the tops of trees. Claw marks scratched into the bark of young trees increase in size as the tree grows, sometimes becoming so large that they look as if they were made by an enormous grizzly bear.

As winter approaches, food again becomes scarce and black bears retreat to dens, where they spend the winter snoozing in a lethargic state similar to but not as deep as hibernation. During dormancy a bear's metabolism slows to half its normal rate, its heart rate drops from roughly fifty to fifteen beats per minute, and its body temperature drops by about eight degrees centigrade. Despite these energy-saving adaptations, by spring the bear will have lost as much as forty percent of its body weight.

In early summer, black bears pair up for about a month to mate, after which the fertilized egg remains undeveloped until late fall when a delayed implantation occurs. In her first litter, a sow has only one cub; in subsequent litters she usually has two and occasionally three. The cubs are born in midwinter — hairless, eyes closed and often weighing as little as two hundred grams. Although tiny at birth, the young bears suckle voraciously throughout the rest of the winter, so that by the time they emerge from the den in spring they weigh over two kilograms and are covered by a dense coat of black fur. The cubs remain with their mother for a full year before being driven off by either their mother or her prospective mate. A pair of cubs will sometimes remain together for a second year before striking out on their own.

Young maple forest near the Étienne Brûlé Lookout.

The forest in this photograph is typical of many that have recently been logged. The trees are young and there are few fallen logs on the forest floor. This area was probably cleared of its older growth during the 1930s when the Gatineau Hills were being stripped of their forests for fuel and pulpwood. It was the public outcry in response to this cutting that spurred the creation of Gatineau Park. The elderly pines that grow around the Mackenzie King Estate, and a virgin stand of hardwood forest growing on the east side of King Mountain, provide some indication of what Gatineau Park's forests might have been like when Étienne Brûlé paddled up the Ottawa River in 1610.

Fallen birch among maple saplings.

A process of forest succession is occurring around many old fields in Gatineau Park. Around the outer edge of the fields are fast-growing trees, such as aspen and birch, that thrive in direct sunlight. Once these trees become established, they provide a lightly shaded environment in which their own seedlings, but also the seedlings of maple and beech, can grow. At first the maple and beech are few in number, but, as they mature, the shade they provide encourages the growth of their own seedlings while inhibiting the growth of young birch and aspen. Soon the maple and beech completely shade out the aspen and birch.

Sunlight reflecting off the surface of a stream.

I had been sitting beside this stream on the Eardley Escarpment for several minutes before I noticed that sunlight, reflecting off the water's surface, appeared to form lines that existed for only a fraction of a second as the water moved passed. A relatively long exposure exaggerated the effect as it appeared to the naked eye but created a more expressive photograph.

Sunlight and dew-covered grass.

For a few brief moments, as the morning sun peaks over the horizon, a dew-covered field becomes a jewel-clad forest in a far-off world. Out-of-focus water droplets create circles of light and beautiful prismatic effects. Even the slightest shift in focus or camera position radically alters the effect, transporting the viewer into strange new worlds.

White birch in abandoned farm field beside Notch Road.

In many winter scenes, an absence of bright colours reduces compositional elements to line, shape and subtle variations of tone. In this photograph, the bright white of fresh snow delineates the horizontal and diagonal lines formed by branches of the birch tree, causing them to stand out from the vertical lines and dark mass of the forest behind them.

Asters, agrimony and hoar frost.

During the day, sunlight warms the earth. After the sun sets, the ground cools and water vapour, suspended in the air, condenses to form dew. When air cools rapidly to below freezing, as it often does on clear nights in autumn, moisture in the air condenses directly from a vapour to hoar frost—delicate needlelike crystals that carpet the landscape.

Archway on the shore of Pink Lake.

The soft rock around the shore of Pink Lake is rich in phosphate, a natural fertilizer. During the 1970s, the wear and tear of thousands of visitors walking around Pink Lake speeded up erosion of the bedrock, causing large amounts of phosphate to drain into the lake, where it encouraged the growth of microscopic algae. In summer the large numbers of algae give Pink Lake a green cast; they also consume so much oxygen that they threaten to upset the lake's ecological balance. During the 1980s, a rehabilitation campaign was undertaken to curtail phosphate contamination. Thousands of trees were planted around the lake to reduce erosion, and pathways and boardwalks were built to minimize visitor impact.

Cecropia moth larva on glossy buckthorn beside Pink Lake.

In early spring, several weeks before this photograph was taken, a female cecropia moth emerged from a cocoon, mated and deposited a small cluster of eggs on the underside of a leaf. Ten to twelve days later, several tiny larvae emerged. This larva has been eating voraciously and is now fully grown. If it does not fall prey to a bird or to parasites, this caterpillar will soon wrap itself in a silken cocoon and emerge in spring as an adult moth ready to repeat the cycle.

Red oak leaf near Luskville Falls.

Red oak grow throughout the sugar maple-beech forest that dominates Gatineau Park, although red oak requires considerably more sunlight than do maple or beech. As this forest matures, its canopy will thicken and eventually shade out all but the hardiest of the oaks.

Red oak, beech and staghorn sumac on the Eardley Escarpment.

The south-facing slopes of the Eardley Escarpment support a hot, dry micro-climate that is strikingly different from the rest of the park. Here, red oak flourish in an open forest alongside southern species such as white oak, hackberry and red juniper.

WHITE-TAILED DEER

Holding each branch carefully out of the way and placing each step gently on the ground, I crept silently through the forest. It had rained throughout the night; water still dripped from every leaf and branch and a rich odour of wet mulch filled the air. I came to the edge of a field and paused. My timing was perfect; soon the first light of day would strike this field and I would be ready. As I stepped out of the forest, something moved. I couldn't see it, but I knew that only a few steps away something was staring at me through the darkness. I stood motionless for a long time. Ever so slowly the sun crept closer to the horizon and the light of dawn filtered through the mist, gradually revealing the outline of a white-tailed deer. It was a large buck and it stood alert, steam rising from its nostrils as it searched the air for my scent. For a long time we stared at each other. Finally I could restrain myself no longer. Almost imperceptibly, I began to lift my hand toward my camera. The instant I moved, the deer turned, flashed the white underside of its tail, and in one herculean leap sailed several metres across the field and disappeared into the mist.

Why an animal that relies on concealment and fleet of foot for safety would signal to its predators with a white flag is a mystery. However, this is exactly what the white-tailed deer does when it feels threatened and turns to run. It has been suggested that displaying the white underside of its tail is the deer's way of alerting other deer to the presence of danger. However, since the flag is directed toward the predator, and not to

other deer, a more plausible explanation may be that it is an attempt to discourage chase by signalling to the predator that it has been spotted and stands little chance of catching up. The fact that deer flash their tails even when no other deer are present, and the fact that when a chase does occur their tails quickly drop, add credibility to this latter theory.

Gatineau Park's mixture of hardwood forests, beaver meadows and old farm fields is ideal habitat for white-tailed deer. Despite their wariness of humans, they are often sighted in fields bordering the parkways, where they feed intensely around dawn and dusk before retiring to bedding areas within the forest to regurgitate and rechew their food.

A network of trails links bedding and feeding areas year-round but becomes most obvious in winter when deer congregate among stands of pine, spruce and fir. These conifers provide protection from wind and ample foliage upon which to browse, but as winter progresses and the snow cover deepens, many deer leave these areas to congregate on the Eardley Escarpment. The escarpment's southern exposure results in a shallower snow cover, allowing the deer greater freedom to move about.

Most of the year, male and female deer travel in separate small groups, bucks with other bucks, and does with other does and their yearlings and fawns. In early autumn, however, the male groups break up in preparation for the rut. If you look carefully along deer trails at this time of year, you may find triangular patches of disturbed earth where a buck has scraped the ground with his hooves. After scraping, the buck brings his hind legs forward and urinates, allowing urine to run over glands on the back of his legs and carry his scent to the ground, leaving a territorial signpost to warn off intruding males and to announce his presence to any prospective mates.

The rut usually occurs during the second and third week of November and fawns are born between mid-May and mid-June. At birth they have a reddish coat covered in light spots that blends in well with the sun-dappled forest floor. Since they give off almost no odour, their best defence against predators is to lie still and rely on their camouflage to conceal them. They remain close to their birth place for about a month, lying hidden among the surrounding grass or shrubs, while their mother remains nearby, returning often to nurse. In August and September, mother and fawn rejoin their group. Although bucks shed their antlers each winter, the antlers are rarely found; being rich in nutrients, they are quickly consumed by rodents such as mice, voles and squirrels.

Daffodil leaves beside the Fairy Lake Parkway.

Many of my favourite photographs are highly interpretive. Rather than documenting the literal appearance of an object, they present an image that is dynamic and evocative, even though its original subject may not be immediately recognizable. In this image, a lack of sharp focus allows the viewer's eye to wander, while causing sharply defined lines and hues to merge. Almost in spite of the original subject matter, the leaves swirl and the entire picture is filled with motion.

Garden lupin near Lac Philippe.

After taking several broad, rather banal, scenic photographs of this field of lupines, I crouched down among the grass and flowers and began to search out less conventional but, I hoped, more evocative images. In this photograph we see the field as it might have appeared to a snowshoe hare quietly contemplating its next meal. Even with practice it is difficult to previsualize images like these. Instead they are "discovered" while exploring the world through a camera lens.

Fern and lichen-covered rock on the Eardley Escarpment.

Lichens are made up of fungi and algae living in symbiotic association. Through the magic of photosynthesis, the algae produce organic matter upon which the fungus feeds. The fungus produces acids that break down and release nutrients from the rock to which it adheres, and provides physical structure to the lichen, exposing the algae to sunlight like the leaves of a tree.

Interrupted ferns in a field near Kingsmere.

Interrupted fern is a rugged plant that grows in a wide variety of soil conditions. It is found throughout Gatineau Park but is most common at the forest edge around old fields and roadsides, where its fiddleheads are among the earliest of the ferns to emerge in spring. Although they currently make up only a small proportion of the floral kingdom, ferns historically have been among the most successful plants. Three hundred million years ago, enormous insects, including a primitive dragonfly with a wingspan over a metre across, lived in junglelike forests where giant ferns flourished alongside horsetails and clubmosses that grew to heights of nearly forty metres.

Mixed forest near Keogan Lodge.

The amount and quality of sunlight, moisture and soil all influence which species of plants germinate and grow in a particular region. Often even a subtle change in environment results in dramatically different forest types growing in close proximity to one another. The mixed forest of maple, spruce, poplar and pine in this photograph grows on a north-facing slope only a short distance from the east-facing sugar maple-beech forest in the opposite photograph. While plants' sensitivity to environmental change encourages diversity within the forest community, it also leaves entire species susceptible to such insidious threats as acid rain and global warming.

Hoar frost covered sugar maple-beech forest.

In recent years, Quebec's magnificent sugar maple forests have experienced a significant decline. While scientists debate the cause (air pollution, acid rain, climatic change, insects and disease are all cited as potential culprits), the maples' rate of growth has dropped by as much as two thirds of what it was during the 1950s, and trees that were once expected to live for centuries are beginning to die back at as early as seventy-five years of age.

Ladybird beetle on flower spike of timothy grass.

Ladybird beetles, often called ladybugs, feed on mites, aphids and other insects, many of which are injurious to plants. For this reason they are sometimes introduced to orchards as a means of combating insect infestations. Like many plants that grow in open fields, grasses are pollinated by wind. If you walk through a field of timothy grass at just the right time in late summer, each stalk you touch will waver in the air, releasing a cloud of thousands of tiny, yellow pollen grains from its flower spike.

Spider web on teasel.

The hole in this web, directly beneath the spider, was probably created by an insect who became trapped in the web and then either struggled free or, more likely, was killed, drained of its nourishment, and then cut loose by the spider. Some spiders repair such breaks, others simply cut the entire web loose and build a new one as it becomes worn.

BLACK-CAPPED CHICKADEE

I remember clearly one particular ski trip in Gatineau Park when I was a child. On this day, someone put a pile of sunflower seeds in my hand and instructed me to hold them out for the birds who were flying all around us. Minutes passed, an eternity to a child, and nothing happened. My arm began to tire. Then suddenly, out of nowhere, a mass of feathers exploded beside my head and a wonderful little creature was digging its tiny claws into my fingertips. Soon there was another bird and another after that, and there have been countless others since. To this day, I carry with me a small bag of seeds whenever I go skiing, and I doubt I will ever tire of the delightful sensation of a chickadee scrambling about on my fingertips while it picks its choice of seeds from my outstretched hand.

Throughout winter the "chicka-dee-dee-dee" song of the black-capped chickadee is a constant presence around birdfeeders at ski lodges throughout Gatineau Park. When the snow is gone, and skiers are no longer around to refill the bird feeders, chickadees flit from tree to tree eating seeds, nuts and fruit, often poking their heads into cracks in the bark or inside cones looking for insects and their eggs.

In spring, male chickadees begin to whistle a high-note low-note "fee-bee" song as the flocks break up into mating pairs that become increasingly intolerant of other birds. Soon, each pair excavates a nest, usually within three metres of the ground in the soft wood of a decaying birch or pine. Occasionally a pair will take up residence inside an old woodpecker's hole. Unlike woodpeckers, who leave a substantial pile of wood chips at the base of a tree, chickadees remove the debris they excavate, carrying hundreds of tiny wood chips from the nest site to nearby perches before dropping them to the ground.

Inside the tree, the female lays six to eight dull white eggs with reddish brown spots in a warm bed of moss, animal hairs, feathers, insect cocoons or other soft materials. During incubation the male brings food to a perch near the nest and gives a soft "fee-bee" call. The female emerges, takes the food, gestures with a quivering of her wings and a soft "teeship" call and then returns to the nest to eat. After the chicks have hatched, the male brings food directly to the young, and within a few days the chicks are strong enough to be left on their own and the female joins her mate in gathering food. The young leave the nest roughly sixteen days after hatching but continue to be fed by their parents for another two weeks. After that they leave their parents, but continue playfully to harass and chase one another for several more days.

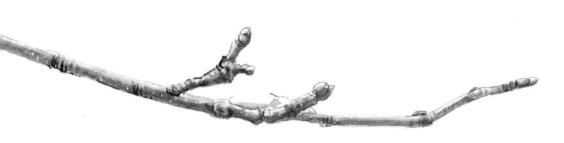

Mushroom cluster on a dead tree.

The presence of mushrooms on the forest floor is evidence of an extensive subterranean network of hairlike filaments or *mycelia* — the body of a fungus. The mushrooms themselves are the reproductive structures of the fungus, serving a function similar to that of the flowers of a flowering plant. While flowers produce fruit and seeds, mushrooms produce spores — the reproductive cells of fungi. The white, powdery substance in this photograph is composed of thousands of tiny spores that have fallen from the gills of the mushroom.

Sulphur shelf fungi on a sugar maple near Bourgeois Lake.

Fungi generally feed on dead organic matter. This sulphur shelf fungus also feeds on living tissue and, in doing so, will accelerate the death and decomposition of this tree. Although parts of a fungus may die, a single specimen may continue to reproduce itself for thousands of years, spreading its tiny filaments over many hectares of forest.

West wall of the Abbey Ruin at the Mackenzie King Estate.

Between 1935 and 1937 William Lyon Mackenzie King had several ruins erected around the grounds of his Kingsmere Estate. This corner wall, containing a window and doorway, was made from stone he retrieved from a house that was being demolished on Daly Avenue in Ottawa. It stands beside a large bay window frame, retrieved from the same Daly Avenue house, and two walls made from stone salvaged from the burned debris of the original Parliament Buildings.

Stream beside the Waterfall Trail near the Mackenzie King Estate.

King had a romantic view of country life and took great pleasure in "beautifying" nature by cleaning up the forest and building walkways and gardens. The Waterfall Trail, which meanders alongside this stream from the Mackenzie King Estate to Bridal Veil Falls, was one of his favourite walks. Not surprisingly, King was outraged when his neighbour Basil Mulvihill dammed this stream in 1948 and used a bulldozer to beautify his own bit of land, carving out the depression that forms Mulvihill Lake. The Larriault Trail, which begins at the Mulvihill Lake parking lot on the Champlain Parkway, offers an alternate route to Bridal Veil Falls, as well as an excellent overview of the Ottawa River Valley.

Sunlight and cloud formations, Champlain Lookout.

Only a small proportion of sunlight that strikes Earth's atmosphere actually reaches the planet's surface. Most is either reflected back into space or is absorbed as it passes through the atmosphere. The shorter blue-violet wavelengths of light are absorbed to a greater degree than the longer yellow and orange wavelengths. Consequently, early and late in the day when the sun is close to the horizon, and sunlight passes through the atmosphere obliquely, a greater proportion of blue-violet light is absorbed and sunlight takes on warm yellow and orange hues.

Ice-covered beech tree near Black Lake.

A heavy frost followed by several hours of freezing rain has transformed this beech tree into an enchanting ice sculpture. The fuzzy husks of beech nuts still cling to several branches, although their cargo has long since dropped to the ground. Very often it is "bad" weather — thunder storms, freezing rain — that creates opportunities for dramatic and compelling photographs — photographs that awaken within us a sense of wonder and an appreciation of the beauty of the natural world.

Crab spider on a bull thistle.

Crab spiders hunt by lying in wait on flower blossoms, ready to ambush insects that come in search of nectar. This spider appears to have lost a leg, possibly during a struggle to overcome its prey. The leaves, stems and even the flower heads of bull thistle are protected from grazing animals by thousands of sharp spines. This flower head has only just begun to bloom. Soon its protective cover will split open and divide into an array of spiny bracts encircling the base of the flower. Within a few weeks, the flower head will transform into a bundle of seeds, each one attached to a parachute of silken filaments that will be carried into the air by an autumn breeze.

Wild columbine on a granite outcrop in the forest.

Wild columbine thrives in the open sunshine and well drained sandy soil on the Eardley Escarpment and on many rocky outcrops throughout Gatineau Park. It blooms in early summer and is often pollinated by humming birds and long-tongued bees that feed on the generous supply of nectar in the tall spurs rising up the back of the petals.

Tree swallow beneath the Eardley Escarpment.

When I first caught sight of this tree swallow, it was darting back and forth above a field searching for insects. After awhile I noticed that it kept returning to perch close to one of the bird boxes erected on fence posts around the field. Being careful not to approach so close that I upset the bird or its mate, I set up my camera and tripod a few metres from the nest and waited for the bird to come and investigate its new neighbour. At first the swallow seemed oblivious to my presence, but suddenly it veered to one side and alighted on the fence nearby. I quickly focused and took this picture. Within seconds, its curiosity satisfied, the bird was once again hunting for insects above the field.

Eastern hemlock and granite cliff behind Willson House, Meech Lake.

Thomas "Carbide" Willson created this pond by damming a small stream that flowed through the woods behind his house. One day as I walked past this spot, I stopped to watch a great blue heron on the opposite shore. Later in the day, I passed by again and was surprised to see that the heron had not moved. It stood exactly as I had left it, poised as if it were about to strike at some unsuspecting prey. Several days later, I walked by here again and the heron had still not moved. This time I unpacked my telephoto lens and set up my camera to have a closer look. The heron, as it turned out, was nothing more than the weathered roots of an ancient pine.

GREAT BLUE HERON

The great blue heron is a magnificent bird. Standing well over a metre high, with a two-metre wingspan, it has a beautiful greyish blue plumage accented by long white feathers around the head and touches of white and cinnamon along the neck. Despite its size, the heron can lift itself from the water with uncanny grace and is a delight to watch as it circles with a slow rhythmic movement of its wings, gradually gaining altitude until it clears the forest canopy and flies away. Often when I have been walking through the woods and have disturbed a heron, it has not been the bird's movements that have alerted me to its presence, but the unmistakable slow, rhythmic sound of those huge wings moving overhead.

The herons arrive in Gatineau Park in late March and early April. They build their nests, platforms of sticks sometimes over a metre across, in the upper branches of trees, usually in colonies in swamps or beaver ponds where water surrounds the base of the tree, possibly because of the protection it affords against predators. In April or May, the female lays from three to five pale greenish-blue eggs on a bed of fine twigs, leaves, pine needles, moss and grass. The eggs are incubated for about twenty-eight days, during which time they are rotated about once every two hours. Great blue herons lay their eggs at least two days apart, resulting in a spread of several days between hatching of the first and last chicks. Consequently, when food is scarce, the last chick to hatch often does not grow strong enough to compete for food among its siblings and eventually dies of starvation. Within two months of hatching, the young begin flying recklessly around the colony and soon after abandon the nest.

At any time of day, but particularly at dawn and dusk, great blue herons can be seen standing motionless or stalking through the shallow waters of ponds and streams — waiting for unsuspecting prey to pass within reach of their sharp, pointed bills. They eat fish, frogs, snakes, salamanders, grasshoppers and other insects, as well as small rodents such as mice and shrews.

The colonies disperse in late summer, but the fall migration does not begin until mid-September, and some birds remain in the park well into October. Others that have nested farther north may also stop in the park to feed and rest before moving on to their winter homes in the southern United States, Mexico and Central America.

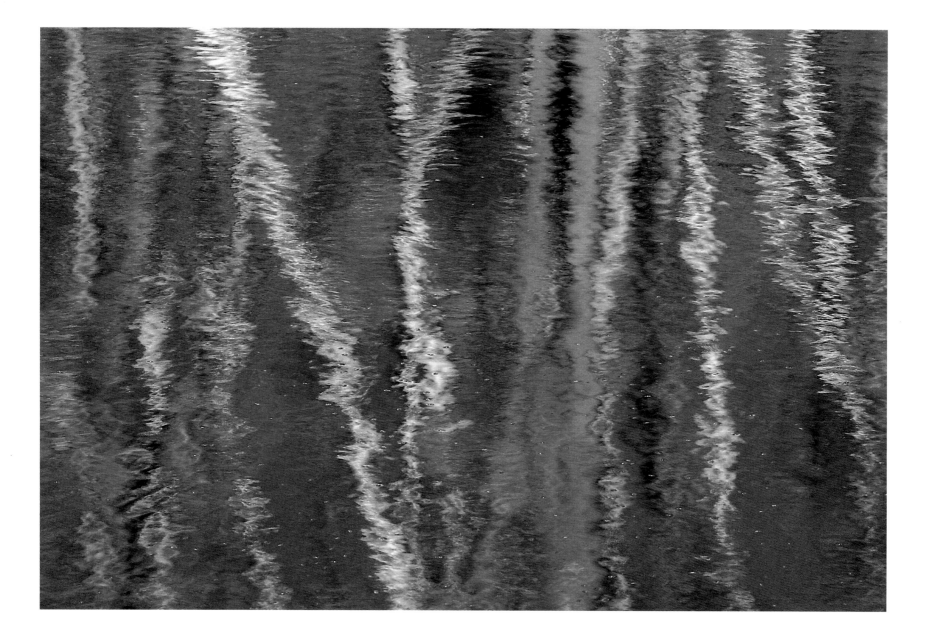

Maple and birch reflections in a beaver pond in autumn.

The reflections that I find most interesting to photograph are not the typical sharp, picture-postcard images of snow-clad mountains, but rather the less distinct reflections created when the water's surface is disturbed. Each slight breeze or tossed pebble distorts the water's surface in a different way, creating unique kaleidoscopic effects. Throughout most of the day, the vantage point from which this photograph was taken offers a clear view of the sticks and mud that rest on the bottom of the pond. However, for a short period each morning, if the sky is not overcast, sunshine pierces through an opening in the forest and illuminates the maple and birch trees that grow on the steep bank of the opposite shore, creating intense reflections on the water's surface.

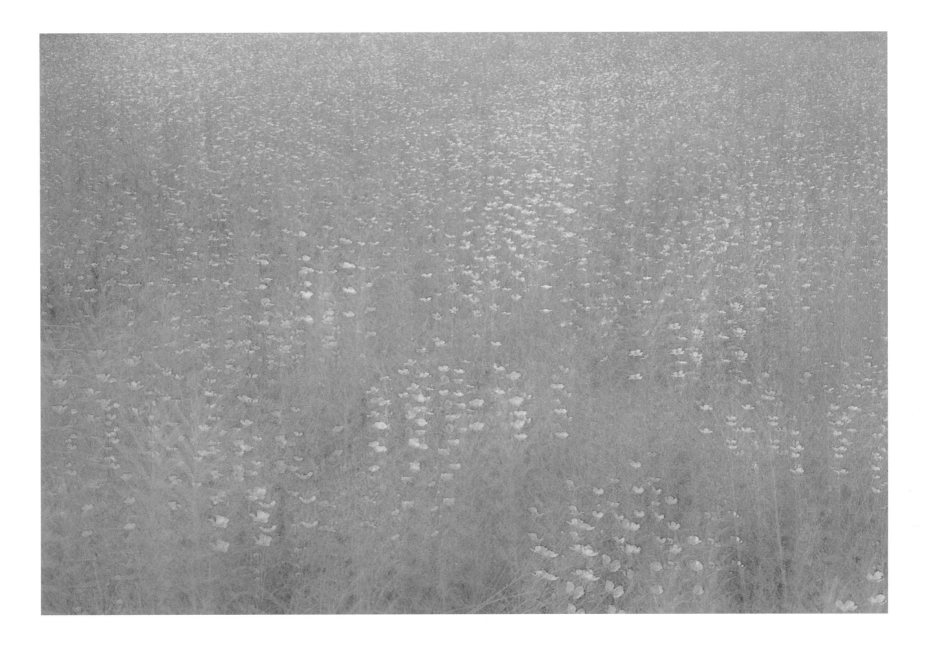

Buttercups and cow vetch in a field near Meech Lake.

At times it can be difficult to convey the impression of a landscape within the confines of a small, two-dimensional picture space. In creating this photograph I wanted to convey some sense of the vast expanse of flowers that grew throughout the field. A wide angle lens was necessary to include the entire field within the picture but had the effect of making most of the flowers appear distant and insignificant. I tried framing compositions of parts of the field, but found they did not convey the impression I was looking for. Eventually I settled on a composite image, making several exposures on a single piece of film, each at a slightly different camera angle.

American toadlet beside Ridge Road.

Had it not suddenly leapt out of my way, I would certainly have not seen this young toad hidden among the litter of leaves on the forest floor. Even as a full-grown adult, several times its current size, this toad will blend into its environment so well that it will be difficult to spot unless it moves. If their camouflage fails, toads have a backup defence against predators: toads' warts, and glands behind their ears, produce a foul tasting poison that usually discourages even the hungriest of predators.

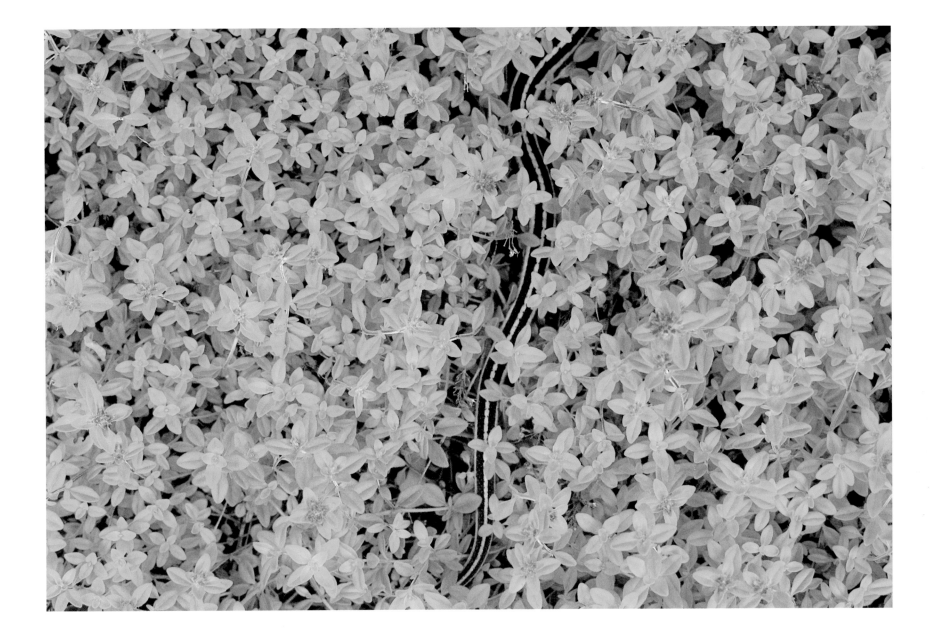

Eastern garter snake in heal-all.

Garter snakes are one of the few animals that are immune to the toxins exuded by toads. In early summer, as toads complete their transformation from tadpoles to toadlets and emerge from ponds, garter snakes have been seen moving slowly along the shoreline, eating every third or fourth toadlet that hopped by. Some predatory birds have learned to eat toads without consuming the skin, thus avoiding the toxin.

Squirrel tracks and beech tree north of Harrington Lake.

The tracks in this photograph were made by either a red or a grey squirrel, both of which are common throughout Gatineau Park. Northern flying squirrels also inhabit the park, although, because they are nocturnal, they are seldom seen. Flying squirrels glide from tree to tree with the aid of large flaps of skin that extend from their wrists to their ankles. They can turn sharply in midflight, manoeuvre around a tree or other obstacle, and pull up to alight on a branch like a bird. If, on the morning after a fresh snow, you come across a set of squirrel tracks that begins in a clearing and runs directly to the nearest tree, you can be fairly certain they were made by a northern flying squirrel.

Young beech trees near the Hickory Trail.

To ensure a steady food supply throughout the winter, red squirrels store nuts and seeds in large underground caches. They also store mushrooms, which they hang up to dry in the upper branches of trees until they are ready to be cached. Grey squirrels, on the other hand, bury individual nuts throughout the forest. In winter I have often come across grey squirrel tracks that lead from the base of a tree to a small tunnel dug in the snow. Usually the tunnel is littered with pieces of dry leaves and bits of acorn husk or the scales of a pine cone. Throughout their lives, the beech trees in this photograph will produce thousands of nuts. Some of these will be buried by grey squirrels, and, of these, roughly fifteen percent will never be retrieved. These few nuts, because they have been so carefully planted, stand a good chance of taking root and becoming the next generation of forest.

Red maple, oak and white pine on King Mountain.

A hike around King Mountain offers a first-hand look at the diversity of Gatineau Park's forests. A small stand of hemlocks, an open oak forest, a few majestic pines and a virgin stand of maple and beech, including trees that are over two hundred years old, can all be seen within a few minutes' walk from the Black Lake parking lot beside the Champlain Parkway.

Ice-covered forest viewed from atop King Mountain.

A midwinter storm has doused this hillside with freezing rain, leaving a heavy burden on the branches of a solitary white pine. Landscapes change dramatically through the seasons, but also from one day to the next, particularly in spring when new growth surges forth as if released from a floodgate. In May, flowers, leaves and buds transform this hillside, almost overnight, into a tapestry of pale green, yellow and white against the mottled brown background of tree trunks and dry leaves.

RACCOON

Raccoons are familiar visitors around the scenic lookouts and picnic grounds in Gatineau Park. Displaying a simultaneously bold but wary disposition, and wearing distinctive black masks, they sneak about like little bandits, sifting through garbage bins in search of food. Generally solitary, raccoons are most active at night, travelling within a home range that varies in size depending on the availability of food. Their diet is remarkably diverse; apart from whatever human garbage they can find, they eat carrion, worms, birds' eggs, small mammals, frogs and even turtles and turtle eggs. With their front paws, which are extraordinarily humanlike in appearance and dexterity, they feel for crayfish, slugs and snails hidden among rocks and mud in shallow waters of lakeshores and streams. In autumn they also eat a tremendous volume of nuts and fruit, as much as doubling their weight in preparation for winter.

In November, Gatineau Park's ponds and streams freeze over, food becomes scarce, and raccoons seek shelter from the cold inside dens, often in hollow logs, rock piles or abandoned burrows. They may emerge occasionally to feed, but for the most part remain in their dens until late winter when the males become restless. Like little Don Juans, they roam the forest searching for the dens of females in estrus, staying with each female for only a few hours. About a month after conception, pregnant females begin to feed more regularly and to search out a suitable birthing den, usually a cavity in a tree that is well protected from the elements and several metres above the ground. As many as seven kits are born in early spring and, although they are only slightly furred at birth, their coats develop quickly, allowing the mother to leave the den for hours at a time to search for food. Soon the young begin to make little growling noises and to poke their heads out of the den. Occasionally one falls to the ground and must be rescued and carried back up by its mother.

As the kits become more active, the mother moves them to a new den near ground level. From here they can pursue their curiosity, venturing out to play and search for food nearby. As soon as the young are strong enough, the entire family leaves the den, and by four months of age the young may roam independently for days at a time. They do not roam far, however, and return to den close by their mother that winter. The following spring the yearlings disperse, often travelling several kilometres before establishing a home range of their own.

One of the most enchanting sights to be seen in Gatineau Park occurs on summer nights around campgrounds at Lac Philippe and Lac la Pêche. From the warmth and safety of their campfires, children can marvel, with trepidation and delight, at what appear to be luminescent jewels floating through the surrounding darkness as the many pairs of eyes of a family of curious raccoons glisten in the light of the fire.

Butter and eggs in a field beside the Gatineau Parkway.

Butter and eggs blooms in colonies along roadsides and in dry fields through mid- and late summer. Its short stalk is covered by small yellow flowers with long basal spurs. Each flower has an orange cap that acts as a landing platform for bumblebees, who extend their tongues deep into the spur in search of nectar.

Cow vetch in a clearing near Pink Lake.

Like butter and eggs, cow vetch is seen in summer in colonies along roadsides and in dry fields. These photographs present an intimate and unfamiliar view of subjects that we often take for granted. I am sure I have crushed these tiny flowers beneath the soles of my boots and the wheels of my car far more often than I have stopped to admire their delicate beauty.

The Ruins of Thomas Willson's powerhouse and acid condensation tower on Meech Creek.

Thomas Willson was a remarkable inventor and entrepreneur who in 1907 built an elaborate summer home on a clifftop overlooking the east end of Meech Lake. The home, known as Willson House, now serves as the federal government's Meech Lake Conference Centre. In his basement laboratory, Willson produced a revolutionary new superphosphate fertilizer. To test the commercial potential of his discovery, he needed to produce fertilizer by the ton, so, on the site where Little Meech Lake drains into Meech Creek, he built a large-scale experiment — the world's first phosphoric acid condensation plant.

Thomas Willson's powerhouse on Meech Creek.

Willson's experiment was a success and, convinced that he was on the verge of creating an enormous industrial empire, he mortgaged almost everything he owned to bring the fertilizer into large-scale production. The project came to an abrupt end when Willson failed to meet his production deadline and, in one broad sweep, all of his assets were seized. Known locally as "The Mill," the skeletal remains of Willson's ambitious experiment still haunt the shores of Meech Creek — a popular destination for skiers, hikers and sunbathers.

Common cattails in a marsh near Camp Fortune.

Cattails are important to many wildlife species. Each flower spike contains over two hundred thousand seeds, which are eaten by mice and ducks. Red-winged blackbirds and marsh wrens nest among the shelter of cattail leaves, and muskrats and geese feed on their stalks and roots.

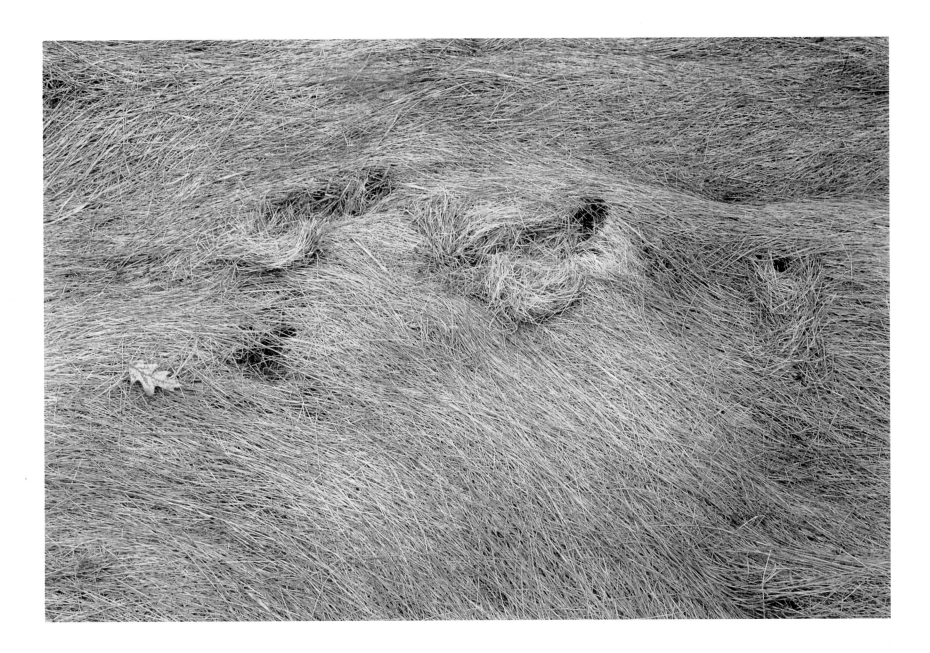

Meadow vole tunnels in a field near Camp Fortune.

Meadow voles are mouselike rodents that live in open woodlands and meadows where tall grass is abundant. They are preyed upon by numerous carnivores including foxes, bobcats, wolves, hawks and owls, so, to survive as a species, they must be extremely prolific. Before it is a year old, a single meadow vole may have as many as forty offspring, who are themselves able to reproduce as early as three weeks of age. This photograph was taken in early spring while the grass was still matted down from the winter's snow.

Tree trunk and broken granitic rock near Luskville Falls.

In composing this photograph, I was simply responding to its strong graphic qualities: the juxtaposition of lines and tones and the contrasting textures of the rock and tree. Later, when I showed the processed film to a friend, he said that to him the photograph suggested solidity and permanence. A few days later I returned to the site to discover that the tree had fallen down. Now when I look at this image I see gaping cracks and the places where pieces of the rock have flaked off, a reminder of the transience of life and the speed with which the forces of erosion alter the landscape.

Stream and lichen-covered rock on the Eardley Escarpment.

The rock over which this stream flows is some of the oldest and most enduring rock on the continent. It was formed hundreds of millions of years ago deep beneath an ancient mountain range. Over time, millions of streams, just like this one, have carried pebbles and particles of stone over the bedrock, gradually wearing the mountains away.

White birch near the Eardley Road.

White birch are common throughout Gatineau Park. Those growing in the forest must compete for sunlight and consequently have long, often crooked trunks with a scattering of branches at the top. The tree in the foreground, which grows on the edge of the forest where sunlight is more plentiful, has a shorter trunk with many branches throughout its entire length. The much larger yellow birch, whose bark becomes scaly or plated as the tree ages, also grows within the park, although it is less common.

Eastern white cedar in a marsh near Pink Lake.

Eastern white cedar thrives in moist soil around lakeshores and in wet, low-lying forest regions like this one near Pink Lake. Cedar is a tough, sinewy wood that is very resistant to decay. Old stone fences and cedar fence rails, littered throughout the forest around Meech Lake and along Ridge Road, are all that remain of the homesteads of pioneers who eked their living from these rocky hills over a century ago.

WOODPECKER

In midwinter the Gatineau forests begin to resonate with the sound of woodpeckers drumming. For woodpeckers, drumming their bills against the sides of trees is akin to the whistles and chirps of songbirds; it is their language, their way of enticing a prospective mate or of asserting their presence in defence of their territory.

Woodpeckers have many other equally extraordinary characteristics. They have short legs that extend into three or four long and very strong toes with sharp, curving claws, a configuration that allows them to grasp onto even the smoothest bark. Using their stiff tail feathers as a brace, they can walk straight up a vertical tree trunk or suspend themselves almost upside down on the underside of a branch. As they scramble up and around the trunks and branches of trees, woodpeckers use their acute hearing to detect their favourite food — insects and their larvae and pupae — gnawing or moving about under bark and within the wood. Once it has located its prey, the woodpecker pecks away with its chisel-like bill until its food is exposed. Repeatedly hammering one's face into solid wood might seem like an odd way to earn a meal; however, the impact of each blow is absorbed by the bird's thick-walled skull, by a thin shock-absorbing space between the outer membrane of the brain and the brain itself, and by strong muscles around the head and neck.

The woodpecker's tongue is also remarkably well adapted to the bird's particular feeding habits. The point of the tongue is barbed, like a harpoon, and is hard and sharp enough to spear large insects. Bristles along the edge of the tongue are coated with sticky saliva to capture ants and other small insects. Unlike most birds, whose tongues are secured in the mouth, a woodpecker's tongue is connected to two semi-elastic cartilaginous horns that wrap around the back of its skull and up over the top of its head, and are anchored inside the right nostril. By sliding this apparatus around its skull, a woodpecker is able to extend its tongue deep into the core of rotten trees where colonies of ants and other insects live.

Woodpeckers excavate roosting cavities throughout their home range, which varies from roughly one hectare for the hairy and downy woodpeckers to as many as eighty hectares for the larger pileated woodpecker. In late winter and spring, mated pairs excavate a nesting cavity high up in a tree. Unlike many other birds, woodpeckers do not line their nests with anything other than a few wood chips leftover from the excavation. The female lays three to five white eggs between late March and the third week of June. Usually the male stays on the eggs at night while his mate sleeps nearby. The young hatch naked and blind, but within three to four weeks are ready to leave the nest. During the last few days before fledging, the chicks make such a racket that they can easily be heard at ground level, several metres from the base of the tree. After leaving the nest, the young continue to be fed by their parents while they learn to find food for themselves. Even then, the family may stay together well into September before the young disperse.

Aster blossoms in a field beside the Gatineau Parkway.

I had stopped here to photograph a bumble bee searching for nectar among these aster blossoms. After the bee flew away, I stayed to photograph the flowers themselves. As I peered through the camera lens, I moved gradually closer to the flowers, all the while growing more and more excited by what I saw. Eventually the flowers disappeared, transformed into a colourful montage of leaves, petals and stems.

Oxeye daisy, buttercup and clover.

This photograph of a summer field was shot through a veil of grass and flower stems. The veil softened sharp contrasts between lines and tones, helping to create a more intimate portrait that underscores the delicate quality of the wildflower petals.

Hoar frost on dried maple leaves.

The environmental conditions that caused condensation to form on these leaves and on the rock opposite were very different. Hoar frost condensed on the leaves when a warm autumn day was followed by a clear night, during which the temperature dropped quickly to below freezing. The rock was subjected to several days of intense cold before being surrounded by a mass of warm, moist air. As warm air passed over the rock's surface, it cooled and was no longer able to hold its moisture, which condensed as tiny water droplets and frost.

Condensation on a glacial erratic.

The glaciers that descended on Gatineau Park during the last ice age carried with them huge volumes of broken rock and earth, which they had scraped off the landscape to the north. When the glaciers retreated, they left this debris behind in the form of moraines, like the one upon which O'Brien Beach is situated at the southeast end of Meech Lake, and in the form of erratic boulders, like this one, scattered throughout the forest.

Red maple at Luskville Falls.

The bark of a young red maple can be as smooth and grey as a beech tree, but everything else about the red maple is red: its buds, its twigs, its flowers and fruit, and its spectacular scarlet leaves in autumn. Red maple, sometimes called swamp or water maple, requires considerably more water than the more common sugar maple. It is often found growing on the banks of streams, like this one on the Eardley Escarpment, or where water pools in low-lying areas throughout the park.

Red maple sapling with white pine needles.

This red maple sapling has found ideal conditions in which to take root — a shaded rock crevice where meltwater and rain collect in rich soil. However, as the tree grows, the surrounding rock will limit the spreading of its roots so that, while the tree may live a long and healthy life, it will remain relatively small. At the base of the Eardley Escarpment, where the soil is both rich and deep, a few mature red maples have grown to their full potential, with trunks approaching a metre in diameter.

Trout lily leaves and birch bark.

Each year a new layer of leaves, twigs and other litter collects on the forest floor. This organic material contains potential food energy for the insects, fungi, bacteria and protozoa that inhabit the soil. The soil dwellers are the recyclers of the forest ecosystem; they break down complex proteins and carbohydrates of formerly living things into simpler molecular structures that can be reabsorbed into the next generation of forest plants.

Trout lily near Lac Philippe.

As soon as the snow melts and sunlight reaches the forest floor in April, spring beauties, trout lilies, bloodroot and other wildflowers begin to emerge from beneath the carpet of fallen twigs and dry leaves. These plants thrive in the sugar maple-beech forest by blooming early in the year, before the forest canopy blocks out the sunshine.

PORCUPINE

The presence of porcupines in Gatineau Park becomes most obvious in late October when enough leaves have fallen to provide a clear view of the upper branches of trees. At this time of year, porcupines are easily sighted climbing along the trunks and branches of trees eating sapwood and bark. Often they completely strip a tree of its bark, leaving only a white skeleton that stands out like a beacon against the dark mass of the forest.

Since porcupines are most conspicuous in autumn, it is not surprising that many of us assume that they spend most of their time in trees. However, this is not true. Throughout the spring, summer and early fall, porcupines feed on a wide assortment of vegetation, including grass, leaves, twigs, shrubs, flowers and nuts. Often they wade or swim along the shores of ponds, eating water-lilies and pondweeds. They spend the winter in small caves and among rock piles, emerging occasionally to feed on the bark of nearby trees. These dens can easily be identified as the home of a porcupine by the large piles of scat that accumulate inside and around the entrance.

Porcupines are among the most lackadaisical animals in the forest. They rarely travel far, and they never travel fast. A porcupine's full-out run looks, for all its earnestness, like little more than an aggressive waddle. The porcupine, however, can afford to appear lazy; its scientific name, *Erethizon dorsatum*, translates loosely as "the animal with the irritating back." Mixed in amongst a dense coat of hair on their shoulders, back and upper side of their tails are roughly thirty thousand sharply pointed quills that provide a formidable defence against predators. When threatened, a porcupine turns its back to its attacker, often burying its head against a tree or other protection, and thrashes its tail in defence. If the attacker strikes, quills easily penetrate its skin and detach from the porcupine. Inside the attacker, barbs along the side of the quill begin to swell and, as the surrounding muscles expand and contract, the quill is pulled inwards by as much as an inch a day. If the quill penetrates a vital organ the animal may die, or, more commonly, if enough quills become embedded around the attacker's mouth to interfere with eating, the animal eventually starves to death.

The porcupine's defences, however, are not infallible. A fisher is easily able to outmanoeuvre a porcupine and can kill it by biting incessantly at its head. Once the porcupine is dead, the fisher rolls it over and devours it through its soft underbelly. Great horned owls have also been known to kill porcupines by driving their talons through their victim's eye socket into its brain.

During the brief late summer mating season, spine chilling screams pierce the forest as male porcupines battle over females, viciously biting and driving quills into one another. Porcupines are adept at removing foreign quills by grasping them in their mouth and forepaws. Females give birth to only one offspring each year, after a gestation period of nearly seven months, a remarkably long time compared with that of other rodents. Consequently, the newborn porcupine is very well developed — it weighs twice as much as a newborn black bear cub. Its eyes are open, and within hours its quills have dried and are functional. The young porcupine will stay with its mother for only a few weeks while it nurses and plays, learning important survival skills as it scurries about, dodging, erecting its quills and thrashing its tail at the air.

Cattail leaves and reflections in a beaver pond.

The bright colours reflecting off the surface of this pond are suggestive of warm sun, trees and autumn foliage. They stir our imagination and evoke emotion more powerfully than would a straightforward depiction of the leaves and branches on the opposite bank. The cattails play an important role in this process, providing an object upon which our eyes rest, as well as a familiar context for an otherwise abstract design.

New York aster and sensitive ferns.

Each fall, of the thousands of visitors who flock to the parkways and scenic lookouts in Gatineau Park to marvel at the brightly coloured hillsides of sugar maple and beech, only a few will chance to stop and wander through an old field to discover the pastel blooms of goldenrods and asters, or to witness the brief but wonderful transition of the ferns through myriad shades of yellow, gold and brown.

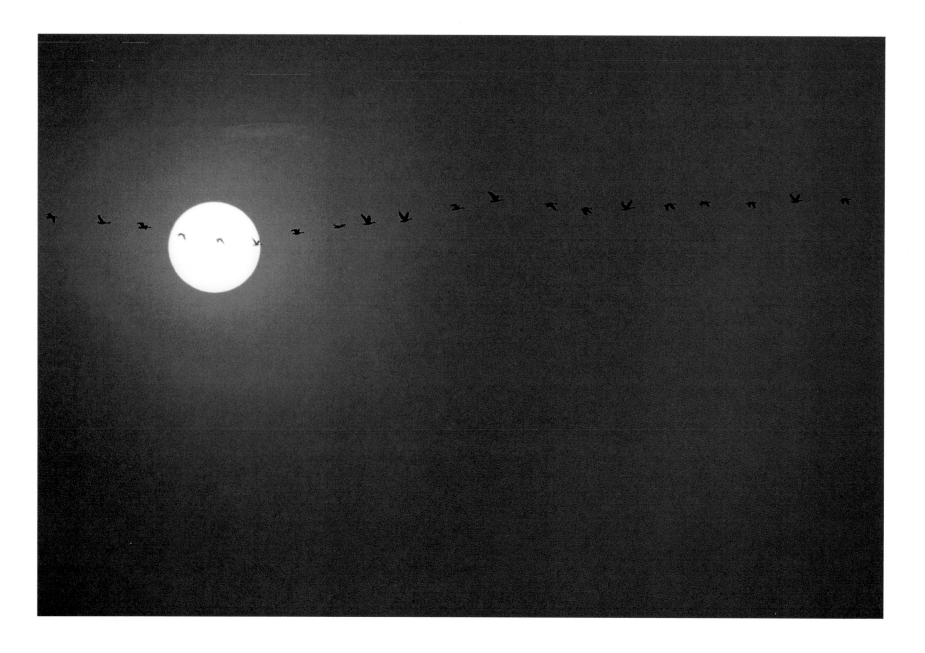

Northern migration of Canada geese.

By flying in a V formation, Canada geese increase the distance they are able to cover between rest stops by as much as seventy percent. Each bird acquires extra lift from vortices of upswelling air rolling off the wing of the bird in front of it. Canada geese are among the few birds that stay together as a family unit once the breeding season has ended. The young hatch on the Arctic tundra in early June and do not leave their parents until the flock returns to the nesting grounds the following spring. During their spring and fall migration, thousands of geese stop to feed and rest in ponds throughout Gatineau Park. This flock was photographed from Champlain Lookout as it approached the Eardley Escarpment from the south.

Black bear claw marks on a beech tree.

In early autumn black bears climb beech trees in search of nuts, leaving deep claw marks in the soft bark. As the tree grows the claw marks grow larger and larger until eventually they look as if they were made by a monstrous grizzly bear. Often black bears sit in the upper branches of beech trees, breaking off nearby limbs and stripping them of nuts. Occasionally these broken branches collect in "bear nests" — piles of branches that look like giant nests in the tops of trees.

Notes

1. E. F. Fowke and R. Johnston, *Folk Songs of Canada* (Waterloo, Ontario: Waterloo Music Company, 1954), p 28.
2. Charles Mortureaux, *Ottawa Ski Club Guide* (Ottawa Ski Club, 1943).
3. Norma Geggie and Stuart Geggie, *Lapêche: A History of the Townships of Wakefield and Masham in the Province of Quebec, 1792 to 1925* (Historical Society of the Gatineau, 1974), p 11.
4. A. B. Robb, *History of Wakefield Village* (Wakefield, Quebec: Wakefield Women's Institute, 1959), p 10.
5. Ibid., p 11.
6. Luke McLuke, "The Sensations of a Sunday Skier," *Ottawa Ski Club News*, no. 9 (February 23, 1927), p 7.
7. Charles Mortureaux, "The Passing of the Eastern Lodge, and the Coming of the Western One," *Ottawa Ski Club News*, no. 1 (December 24, 1930), p 4.
8. W. L. Mackenzie King, "Last Will and Testament of The Right Honourable W. L. Mackenzie King" (Ottawa: Gowling, MacTavish, Watt, Osborne and Henderson, 1950).
9. Canada, *Parliamentary Debates, House of Commons, 6th session*, Vol. 3 (1935), p 3019.

Picture Credits

Page 23   Ivan Kocsis / Ontario Archaeological Society
Page 24   Upper: Ivan Kocsis / Ontario Archaeological Society
            Lower: Alfred Worsley Holdstock / National Archives of Canada / C-40098
Page 25   W. H. Bartlett / National Archives of Canada / C-2303
Page 27   Upper: C. W. Jefferys / National Archives of Canada / C-73702
            Lower: John Macoun / National Archives of Canada / C-11774
Page 28   Archives of Ontario / Acc-11778-4 S16944
Page 29   Upper: Archives of Ontario / Acc-2271 S15154
            Lower: Archives of Ontario / Acc-10010-42
Page 30   Upper: National Archives of Canada / C-6669
            Lower: W. H. Bartlett / National Archives of Canada / C-2401
Page 31   National Archives of Canada / C-25275
Page 33   National Archives of Canada / C-18612
Page 34   National Archives of Canada / C-64876
Page 35   Courtesy of the Historical Society of the Gatineau.
Page 36   National Archives of Canada / C-64877
Page 37   National Archives of Canada / C-38477
Page 38   National Archives of Canada / C-34059
Page 39   Courtesy of the Canadian Ski Museum / 74-39-1-24
Page 41   National Archives of Canada / C-53499
Page 42   Topley / National Archives of Canada / PA-144967
Page 43   National Archives of Canada / C-53492
Page 44   Upper: National Archives of Canada / PA-124444
            Lower: National Archives of Canada / C-46554
Page 45   National Archives of Canada / C-14165
Page 46   Bill Lingard / National Archives of Canada / PA-164433
Page 47   National Archives of Canada / PA-163906

Bibliography

Ballantyne, Bruce. "Up The Line — The Railway From Hull To Maniwaki." *Up the Gatineau!* 17 (1991): 1-4.

Beiser, Arthur, and the Editors of Time-Life Books. *The Earth*. Life Nature Library. New York: Time-Life Books, 1962.

Burbridge, Geof. "A Short History on the Geological History of our Area." *Trail and Landscape* 25, no. 2 (Apr.-June 1991): 47-54.

Burnton, Daniel F., and J. Donald Lafontaine. "An Unusual Escarpment Flora in Western Quebec." *Canadian Field Naturalist* 88 (1974): 337-44.

Canada. *Parliamentary Debates, House of Commons, 6th session.* Vol. 3 (1935): 3019.

Champlain, Samuel de. *The Voyages and Explorations of Samuel de Champlain (1604-1616)*. Translated by Annie Nettleton Bourne. Toronto: Courier Press, 1911.

Cook, Francis R. *Introduction to Canadian Amphibians and Reptiles*. Ottawa: National Museum of Natural Sciences, National Museums of Canada, 1984.

Cranston, J. Herbert. *Étienne Brûlé: Immortal Scoundrel*. Toronto: The Ryerson Press, 1949.

Fletcher, Katharine. *Historical Walks: The Gatineau Park Story*. Ottawa: Chesley House Publications, 1988.

Forsyth, Adrian. *Mammals of the Canadian Wild*. Camden East, Ont.: Camden House Publishing, 1985.

Fowke, E. F., and R. Johnston. *Folk Songs of Canada*. Waterloo, Ontario: Waterloo Music Company, 1954.

Funk, Robert E. "The Laurentian Concept: A Review." *Archaeology of Eastern North America* 16 (1988): 1-38.

Gatineau Park Master Plan. Ottawa: National Capital Commission, 1988.

Geggie, Judith. "Maclaren's General Store Circa 1900: A Sketch." *Up the Gatineau!* 14 (1988): 15-19.

Geggie, Norma. *Wakefield and its People: Tours of the Village*. Ottawa: Chesley House Publications, 1990.

Geggie, Norma and Stuart. *Lapêche: A History of the Townships of Wakefield and Masham in the Province of Quebec, 1792 to 1925*. Historical Society of the Gatineau, 1974.

Gillett, John M., and David J. White. *Checklist of Vascular Plants of the Ottawa-Hull Region*. Ottawa: National Museum of Natural Sciences, National Museums of Canada, 1978.

Godfrey, W. Earl. *The Birds of Canada*. 3d. ed. Ottawa: National Museum of Natural Sciences, National Museums of Canada, 1986.

Harington, C. R. "Quarternary Vertebrate Faunas of Canada and Alaska and their Suggested Chronological Sequence." *Syllogeus 15*. Ottawa: National Museums of Canada, 1978.

Harington, C. R. "The Champlain Sea and its Vertebrate Fauna." *Trail and Landscape* 5, no. 5 (Nov.-Dec. 1971): 137-41.

Hessel, Peter. *The Algonkin Tribe*. Arnprior, Ont.: Kichessippi Books, 1987.

Hogarth, Donald D. "A Guide to the Geology of the Gatineau-Lievre District." *Canadian Field Naturalist* 76, no. 1 (Jan.-Mar. 1962): 1-55.

Hope, Ethel Penman. "Early Settlement of Meech Lake." *Up the Gatineau!* 10 (1984): 20-26.

Hughson, John W., and Courtney C. J. Bond. *Hurling Down the Pine*. 3d ed. Chelsea, Que.: Historical Society of the Gatineau, 1964.

Kricher, John C., and Gordon Morrison. *A Field Guide to Eastern Forests North America*. Peterson Field Guide Series. Boston: Houghton Mifflin Company, 1988.

Likens, Gene E. "Meromictic lake." In *McGraw-Hill Encyclopedia of Environmental Science*, edited by Sybil P. Parker. 5th. ed. New York: McGraw-Hill, 1980.

Mackenzie King, W. L. "Last Will and Testament of The Right Honourable W. L. Mackenzie King." Ottawa: Gowling, MacTavish, Watt, Osborne and Henderson, 1950.

Marshall, Herbert. *History of the Ottawa Ski Club.* N.p., n.d.

Marshall, Herbert. *How Skiing Came to the Gatineau.* N.p., n.d.

McLuke, Luke. "The Sensations of a Sunday Skier." *Ottawa Ski Club News*, no. 9 (Feb. 23, 1927): 7-8.

Meech, Marion A. "Asa Meech." *Up the Gatineau!* 7 (1981): 14-18.

Miller, Frank L. "Distribution and Numbers of White-tailed Deer Wintering in Gatineau Park, Quebec." *Canadian Field Naturalist* 88 (1974): 41-45.

Mortureaux, Charles. "The Passing of the Eastern Lodge, and the Coming of the Western One." *Ottawa Ski Club News*, no. 1 (Dec. 24, 1930): 4.

Mortureaux, Charles. *Ottawa Ski Club Guide.* Ottawa: Ottawa Ski Club, 1943.

Native Trees of Canada. 5th ed. Ottawa: Department of Northern Affairs and Natural Resources, Forestry Branch, 1956.

Parson, Helen E. "Land Use History of the Gatineau Valley 1800-1850." *Up the Gatineau!* 9 (1983): 5-9.

Phillips, R. A. J. *Touring the Two Chelseas.* Chelsea, Quebec: Historical Society of the Gatineau, 1991.

Pielou, E. C. *After the Ice Age: The Return of Life to Glaciated North America.* Chicago: University of Chicago Press, 1991.

Rezendes, Paul. *Tracking and the Art of Seeing: How to Read Animal Tracks and Sign.* Charlotte, Vt.: Camden House Publishing, 1992.

Robb, A. B. *History of Wakefield Village.* Wakefield, Quebec: Wakefield Women's Institute, 1959.

Roberts, Marion. "Carbide Willson — 1860-1915." *Up the Gatineau!* 2 (1976): 16-22.

Stang, Sheila. "The Alexander Story." *Up the Gatineau!* 10 (1984): 4-6.

Stokes, Donald and Lillian. *A Guide to Animal Tracking and Behavior.* Stokes Nature Guides. Boston: Little, Brown and Company, 1986.

Stokes, Donald and Lillian. *A Guide to Bird Behaviour.* Stokes Nature Guides, vols. 1-3. Boston: Little, Brown and Company, 1979, 1983, 1989.

Surficial Geology and the Ice Age in the National Capital Region. Ottawa: Energy Mines and Resources Canada (pamphlet catalogue no. M40-46), 1987.

Terres, John K. *The Audubon Society Encyclopedia of North American Birds.* New York: Wing Books, 1956.

Von Baeyer, Edwinna. *Garden of Dreams: Kingsmere and Mackenzie King.* Toronto: Dundurn Press, 1990.

Willson, Alice E. "A Guide to the Geology of the Ottawa District." *Canadian Field Naturalist* 70, no. 1 (Jan.-Mar. 1956).

Wilson, Roger. *The Land that Never Melts: Auyuittuq National Park.* Toronto: Peter Martin Associates and Ministry of Supply and Services Canada, 1976.

Wright, J. V. *Ontario Prehistory: An Eleven-thousand-year Archaeological Outline.* Ottawa: Archaeological Survey of Canada, National Museum of Man, National Museums of Canada, 1972.

Wright, J. V. *Quebec Prehistory.* Toronto: Archaeological Survey of Canada, National Museum of Man, National Museums of Canada, Van Nostrand Reinhold, 1979.

Wright, J. V. *The Shield Archaic.* Ottawa: National Museums of Canada, 1972.